CONTEMPORARY ART

FROM CRESCENT MOON PUBLISHING

The Art of Andy Goldsworthy: Complete Works: Special Edition
by William Malpas

The Art of Andy Goldsworthy
by William Malpas

Andy Goldsworthy: Touching Nature
by William Malpas

Andy Goldsworthy In Close-Up
by William Malpas

The Art of Richard Long: Complete Works: Special Edition
by William Malpas

Constantin Brancusi: Sculpting the Essence of Things
by James Pearson

Alison Wilding: The Embrace of Sculpture
by Susan Quinnell

Eric Gill: Nuptials of God
by Anthony Hoyland

The Erotic Object: Sexuality in Sculpture
From Prehistory to the Present Day
by Susan Quinnell

Minimal Art and Artists in the 1960s and After
by Laura Garrard

Land Art, Earthworks, Installations, Environments, Sculpture
by William Malpas

Land Art: A Complete Guide to Landscape, Environmental,
Earthworks, Nature, Sculpture and Installation Art
by William Malpas

Richard Long In Close-Up
by William Malpas

Land Art In Close-Up
by William Malpas

Colorfield Painting: Minimal, Cool, Hard Edge, Serial
and Post-Painterly Abstract Art From the Sixties to the Present
by Laura Garrard

Jasper Johns
by L.M. Poole

Frank Stella: American Abstract Artist: Special Edition
by James Pearson

Maurice Sendak and the Art of Children's Book Illustration
by L.M. Poole

The Erotic Object In Close-Up: Sexuality in Sculpture
From Prehistory to the Present Day
By Susan Quinnell

Sacred Gardens: The Garden in Myth, Religion and Art
by Jeremy Mark Robinson

Sex in Art: Pornography and Pleasure in Painting and Sculpture
by Cassidy Hughes

Postwar Art
by George Knighton

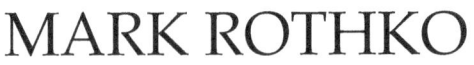

MARK ROTHKO

MARK ROTHKO

The Art of Transcendence

Julia Davis

CRESCENT MOON

First published 1995. Fourth edition 2011. Reprint 2018.
© Julia Davis 2011, 2018.

Printed and bound in the U.S.A.
Set in Book Antiqua 10 on 14pt and Gill Sans.
Designed by Radiance Graphics.

British Library Cataloguing in Publication data

Davis, Julia
Mark Rothko: The Art of Transcendence. – Rev. ed. – (Painters Series)
1. Rothko, Mark – Criticism and interpretation
2. Painting, Modern – 20th century – United States
3. Painting, American
I. Title

759.1'3

ISBN-13 9781861713148 (Pbk)
ISBN-13 9781861713155 (Hbk)
ISBN-13 9781861716774 (Pbk)
ISBN-13 9781861717498 (Pbk)

CRESCENT MOON PUBLISHING
P.O. Box 1312, Maidstone
Kent, ME14 5XU
Great Britain, www.crmoon.com

Contents

Acknowledgements

Pace Gallery, New York. Tate Modern, London.

Thanks to the authors quoted and their publishers, and to copyright owners of the illustrations.

The eye by which I see God is the same as the eye by which God sees me. My eye and God's eye are one and the same – one in seeing, one in knowing, and one in loving.

Meister Eckhart

Anxiety is the dizziness of freedom.

Søren Kirkegaard

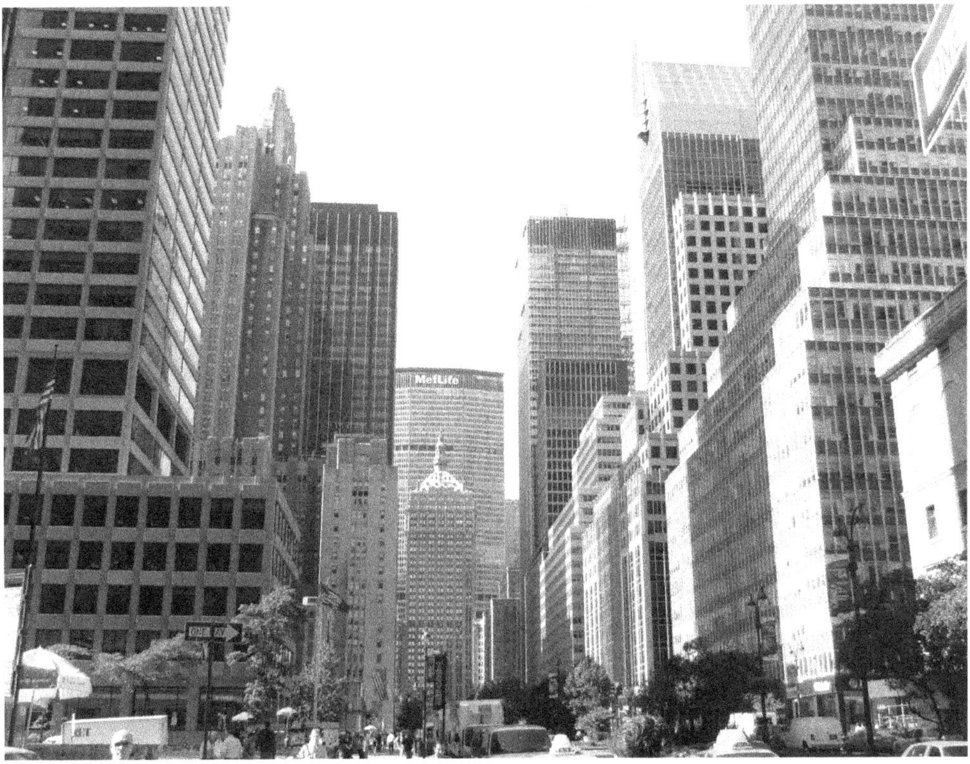

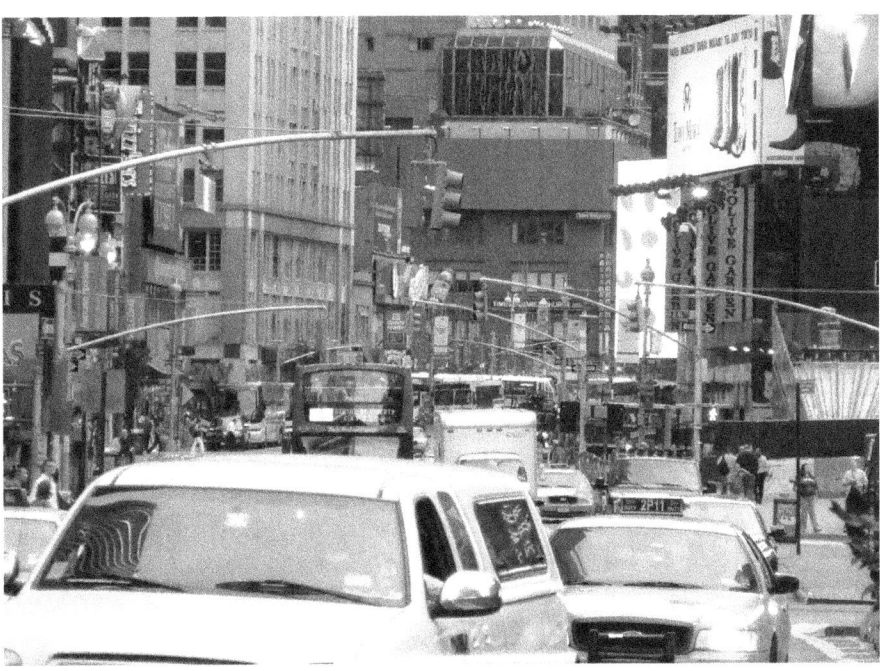

Rothko's city: New York

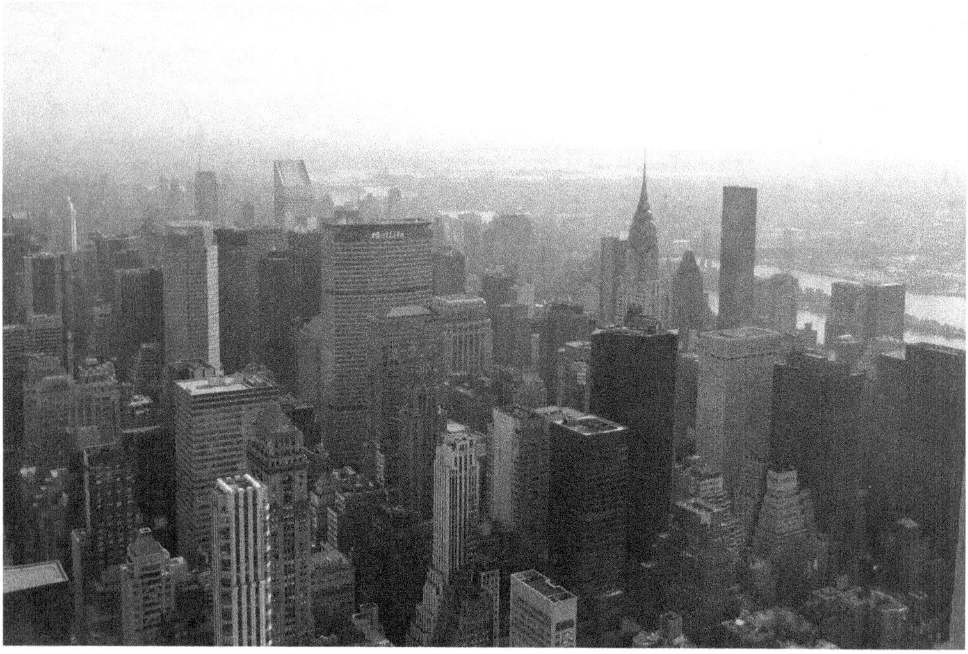

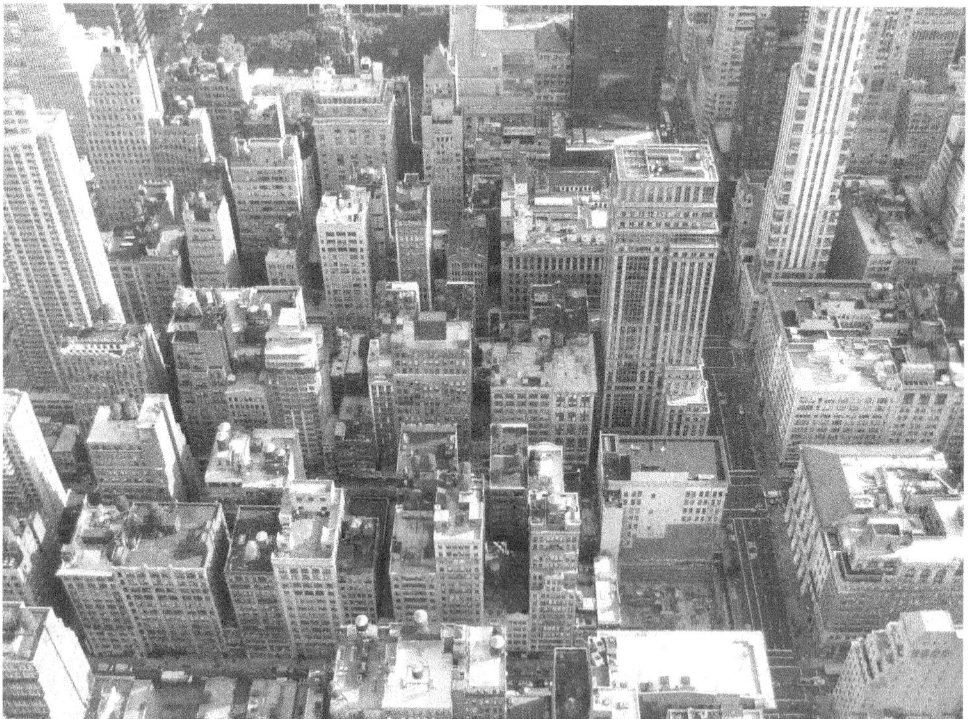

I

INTRODUCTION:
A VERTICAL PORTRAIT
OF THE ARTIST

Art is the proper task of life.

Friedrich Nietzsche

Mark Rothko (September 25, 1903 – February 25, 1970, born Marcus Rothkowitz in Dvinsk, Russia, died in New York City), presents some interesting problems for the art critic. For a start, his art seems to be opaque, ambiguous, effervescent; in short, difficult to write about. In fact, there are many ways of approaching Rothko's paintings. For example, Rothko's art draws on literature, mythology, religion and philosophy, all sorts of discourses that the critic can access and discuss. And Rothko himself talked about his art, in articles, despite maintaining that art is best not discussed and picked over. 'Artists talk in paint – words do not come easily', said Canadian artist Emily Carr.[1]

There is a more challenging consideration for the Rothko art critic, however, and that is the huge amount of material that has grown up around Rothko. Like Vincent van Gogh, Pablo Picasso, Claude Monet and Leonardo da Vinci, Mark Rothko has been lionized by hundreds of art critics. (Of course, there are many that hate him, just as there are those who loathe Monet, Jean-Dominique Ingres, Rembrandt van Rijn's or Andy Warhol. Some of the negative responses to Rothko are discussed here.) Rothko remains, though, a greatly admired painter. His works will not, it seems, reach the same mass audiences as Monet or van Gogh, perhaps because Rothko is an abstract artist, and very few abstract artists achieve the mega-stature of figurative painters such as van Gogh or Monet. True, Picasso has made it into the big time in the art world, but it is Picasso's more palatable, figurative works (such as the nudes) that do the rounds of the fine art print offers or calendars or posters or the limited edition china plate offers in the back of Sunday newspapers. Monet's more 'abstract' waterlilies too have become hugely popular, appearing on teacloths and china plates, but the waterlily paintings are still representational. Abstract art of the Rothko kind – the colorfield skeins of Morris Louis, the black stripes of polychrome shaped canvases of Frank Stella, the bold, black, calligraphic brushstrokes of Franz Kline – has yet to become as widely accepted as Gustav Klimt's nudes or Sandro Botticelli's Madonnas. In the art world itself, though, Mark Rothko is a highly celebrated painter. He appears in the 20th century Olympian pantheon alongside Jackson Pollock, Piet Mondrian, Paul Klee, Robert Rauschenberg and Jasper Johns. (However, Mark Rothko merchandize includes diaries, calendars, posters, tee shirts and mugs. Yep, Rothko mugs and calendars are all very 'serious' and 'tragic' and 'transcendent'. But what's happened with Leonardo and Michelangelo is worse – the images created by those poor devils is plastered on any piece of junk).

One can, if one wishes, connect Mark Rothko's art with a whole welter of art historical references. Rothko can be seen as the inheritor of the European (in particular, the French) tradition, a tradition of painting which exalts the sensuality of colour (Claude Monet, Henri Matisse, Pierre Renoir). Another art historical reading might associate Rothko's late works with the late works of Titian and Rembrandt van Rijn, who tended towards a diffuse, golden light. One might see precursors of Rothko, as Robert Rosenblum does, in J.M.W. Turner's sea-scapes, or the mountains and infinite skies of Caspar David Friedrich.[1]

This view of Mark Rothko as a latter-day Romantic fits in with the associations between Rothko and another Romantic artist named Friedrich – Herr Nietzsche. In this modernist view, Rothko's paintings hark back to Caspar Friedrich's *Monk By the Sea* (1809, Berlin) or *The Traveller* (1817-18, Hamburg), an art of (Christian) Romantic melancholy, infinity and longing.

In poetry, the German Romantic poets – such as Novalis, Johann Wolfgang von Goethe, Heinrich Heine and Friedrich Hölderlin – express this Romantic culture perfectly. In 'In the Morning' ('Des Morgens'), Hölderlin sends out passionate lines to the sky,:

Vom Thaue glänzt der Rasen; beweglicher
  Eilt schon die wache Quelle; die Buche neigt
    Ihr schwankes Haupt und im Geblätter
      Rauscht es und schimmert; und um die grauen

Gewölke streifen röthliche flammen dort,
  Verkündende, sie wallen geräuschlos auf;
    Wie Fluthen am Gestade, woogen
      Höher und höher die Wandelbaren.

Komm nun, o komm, unde eile mir nicht zu schnell,
  Du goldner Tag, zum Gipfel des immels fort!
    Denn offner fliegt, vertrauter dir mein
      Aug, du Freudiger! zu, so lang du

In deiner Schöne jugendlich blikst und noch
  Zu herrlich nicht, zu stolz mor geworden bist;
    Do möchtest immer eilen, könnt ich,
      Göttlicher Wandrer, mit dir!

Des frohen übermüthigen du, daß er
  Dir gleichen möchte; seegne mir lieber dann
    Mein sterblich Thun und heitre wieder
      Gütiger! heute den stillen Pfad mir.

[With dew the lawn is glistening; more nimbly now,
  Awake, the stream speeds onward; the beech inclines
    Her limber head and in the leaves a
      Rustle, a glitter begins; and round the

Grey cloud-banks there a flicker of reddish flames,
  Prophetic ones, flares up and in silence plays;
    Like breakers by the shore they billow
      Higher and higher, the ever-changing.

Now come, O come, and not too impatiently,
  You golden day, speed on to the peaks of heavens!
    For more familiar and more open,
      Glad one, my vision flies up towards you

While youthful in your beauty you gaze and have
  Not grown too glorious, dazzling and proud for me;
    Speed as you will, I'd say, if only
      I could go with you, divinely ranging!

But at my happy arrogance now you smile,
  That would be like you; rather, then, rambler, bless
    My mortal acts, and this day also,
      Kindly one, brighten my quiet pathway.] (93)

Extending the argument further, one can compare the 'paint-theism'[2] of Mark Rothko's canvases with mediæval mysticism, such as Meister Eckhart's (1260-1327) teachings, where the German mystic spoke of sinking down 'from nothingness to nothingness'. Or *The Cloud of Unknowing,* an English 14th century mystical tract, which spoke of the urge to 'smite upon that thick cloud of unknowing with a sharp dart of longing love'. It's too easy, perhaps, to connect the mediæval mystical 'cloud of unknowing', which's associated with the deity, and Rothko's own 'cloud-like' paintings (such as *Light Cloud, Dark Cloud* [private collection], or *Blue Cloud* [1956, Zurich]), products of a different, secular – Godless – age. Rothko was interested in the mystical aura around the gods. His 'clouds' can be seen in this way: as abstract equivalents for the aura surrounding certain divine entities (something like a 20th century abstract equivalent for the halos in mediæval and Renaissance religious art).

The view of Mark Rothko's art as a development from Claude Monet's expansive *Waterlilies* (1916-23), on show at the Orangerie in Paris, or James Whistler's atmospheric waterscapes, is common now. Certainly one can see many correspondences between Monet shrines such as the Orangerie or Giverny and Rothko's Houston Chapel or Tate Gallery room (since opening its modern art building on the South Bank, the Tate Gallery in London has become Tate Modern, with Tate Britain as the older building, which's where the Rothko Room was originally installed).

More recent activity in Mark Rothko's art include the play *Red* by John Logan, which opened in London and transferred to Broadway in 2010; an exhibition of late works at the Tate in London in 2008; a show in Moscow in 2010; and a Rothko canvas broke records at Sotheby's in Gotham when it sold for $72.8 million.

In the discussion that follows I'm concerned more with Mark Rothko's paintings from the 1940s onwards. That is, with Rothko's abstract paintings, not the figurative and semi-abstract pieces work the 1930s. This is a personal choice, in order to analyze a certain area of Rothko's art. The works of the 1920s, 1930s and early 1940s have been dealt with in detail in many studies.[4] I will not be discussing Rothko's many exhibitions, the shows at Betty Parsons Gallery, the Guggenheim or Museum of Modern Art. All that – the significance of Clement Greenberg, Thomas Hess, Harold Rosenberg, Peggy Guggenheim, the *Art of This Century* exhibition, etc – has been discussed elsewhere.

II

MARK ROTHKO CRITICISM

Mark Rothko's art has been seen by critics as 'transcendent' (Ashton, Robertson), 'a sort of spiritual Stonehenge' (Brookner), 'lavish self-indulgence' (Kozloff), 'Dionysian' (R. Hobbs), 'sensuous and spiritual' (Waldman), 'enormous, beautiful, opaque surfaces' (Selz), 'enigmatic, gripping presence' (Goldwater), 'incandescent color' (Greenberg), 'haunting' (Sylvester), 'visionary simplicity' (Sandler) and 'tinted hallucinatory cloth' (de Kooning).[1] For John Ashbery, Rothko 'seems to eliminate criticism'.[2]

The archetypal response to Mark Rothko's art is that it is:

(1) 'heroic',

(2) 'transcendent',

(3) 'spiritual'

and (4) 'tragic' art.

These are four of the most commonly deployed adjectives in Mark Rothko art criticism (others include 'Buddhist', 'Faustian' and 'death-conscious'). Rothko's painting is seen as (1) 'heroic' because it attempts to achieve something great in a world of Existential suffering. Out of the slime and the pain and the horror of modern life rise Rothko's 'heroic' canvases. His canvases become a gesture of affirmation in amongst the global angst (as with Rothko's contemporaries, such as Jackson Pollock and Barnett Newman). Robert Motherwell called large paintings 'heroic'.[3]

Mark Rothko's art is (2) 'transcendent' because it aims to go beyond the usual realms of art, in terms of content and form. It is also religiously transcendent, pointing towards the sort of transcendence that mystics speak of, an ontological and metaphysical transcendence of earthly states.[4] It is Existential because Rothko managed to create something from the Heideggerian state of being 'thrown into the world'. And Rothko's art has many affinities with Existential philosophy (such as Kirkegaardian risk and Sartrean nausea).

Mark Rothko's art is deeply (3) 'spiritual', it seems, because he deals with spiritual matters. Rothko's sense of the spirit and the spiritual dimension informs all of his painting. He is naturally a spiritual or religious painter, like Leonardo da Vinci or Giotto.[5] What comes out of Rothko is nearly always of a spiritual/ religious/ mythological nature. It was the same with painters such as Fra Angelico. Somehow, it seemed as if Fra Angelico could not help painting a Crucifixion or an Annunciate Virgin every time he picked up the brush.

Of course, it was not as simple as that in the world of Italian Renaissance art – there were commissions, patrons to please, economic constraints, a quite different socio-political environment from postwar America. Yet there are significant points of æsthetic and painterly correspondence between the heartfelt religious painters of the Renaissance (and particularly the Trecento and Quattrocento artists such as Cimabue, Duccio di Buoninsegna, Giotto, Masaccio, Simone Martini and Fra Angelico), and postwar painters such as Jackson Pollock, Mark Rothko, Barnett Newman and Brice Marden. Other points of contact for Rothko included masters such as Henri Matisse, of course, and Rembrandt van Rijn.

One can create any 'Mark Rothko' one wishes. If one desires a

Zen Buddhist Rothko, one simply freights one's analysis with discussions of the Buddhist *sunyata* (void) or *nirvana* (desirelessness), relates Rothko's cloud-like canvases to Chinese landscape painting and the Zen Buddhist sparseness of Japanese *haiku* poetry, using quotes from D.T. Suzuki, Alan Watts and the Beat poets. If one fancies an Existential Rothko, one uses Albert Camus, Jean-Paul Sartre, Martin Heidegger, and Søren Kirkegaard as sounding boards (many critics have done this). One can have a Phenomenological Rothko. A Nietzschean Rothko (a popular choice among art critics). A Heideggerian Rothko, ingeniously related by the industrious art critic to Heidegger's *Being and Time* and notions of being, chaos, presence, time, the 'abyss' (*Abgrund*) or 'groundless ground' and so on.[6] One can have a Shakespearean Mark Rothko, who sings the praises of the 'death of God' epoch, a modernist postwar era in which God is dead and everything is rendered meaningless (Camus, Samuel Beckett, Sartre) by the 'terror of history' (Mircea Eliade's term). The critic could load onto the Rothko life-raft theologians such as Karl Barth, Bernard Lonegran, William Johnston, Thomas Merton and of course Teilhard de Chardin. A Rothko for the Death of God Age who nevertheless desperately desires divinity. Happily the critic could muse on the correspondences between the void of Oriental mysticism and the darkness at the heart of an ascetic, monastic, ecstatic kind of Christianity.

One could have a Mediæval Mystical Rothko, a development of the Christian Rothko, in which the darkness of the New York Abstract Expressionist's canvases would be linked to St John of the Cross's 'dark night of the soul', or Meister Eckhart's 'sinking down from nothingness to nothingness'. One could have a Jewish Rothko, ruminating on the Holocaust. One could have a Jungian Rothko, the swimmer in the mythic post-Freudian unconscious, and wielder of mythological archetypes. This Jungian Rothko could happily absorb association with the roster of post-Jungian thinkers (Mircea Eliade, Marie-Louise von Franz, Erich Neumann, Joseph Campbell, William Johnson and Robert Whitmont). Then there is the Literary Rothko, sensitive inheritor of Fyodor Dostoievsky, Knut Hamsun, Franz Kafka, William Shakespeare and Aeschylus.

'Rothko' is so mutable a term or entity, he (it) can be appropriated for any critical ends one cares to name. Michel Foucault, for example, writes: '[i]t is no longer possible to think in our day other than in the void left by man's disappearance.'[7] Mark Rothko, one might claim, is illustrating (equivalents for) this Existential void in his canvases. As Friedrich Nietzsche out it: 'if you gaze for long into an abyss, the abyss gazes also into you'.

One could relate Rothko's near-empty canvases to Fredric Jameson's conception of 'postmodern hyperspace', a space that transcends the human body.[8] This 'hyperspatiality' corresponds to another postmodern concept, the non-place of the (American) desert of Jean Baudrillard.[9] This non-place or void is created by a 'crisis of the master's discourse',[10] of which Rothko's art can be seen as a part. In the non-place or hyperspatial void of post-modern philosophy, words are unwelcome. 'Words, even when they speak of the desert, are always unwelcome,' remarked the French thinker in his dry manner.[11] One recalls Rothko's own antipathy towards words in connection with painting, how words can confuse one's experience of a painting. In the empty space of *chora*, Jacques Derrida said, one can 'avoid speaking'.[12] Mark Rothko's painted voids may be linked to Julia Kristeva's notion of the *chora*, a provisional, fragmentary, ambiguous, marginal, maternal and pre-Oedipal space.[13] For Kristeva, the *chora* is linked to the *avant garde*, modernist project (to writers such as James Joyce, Lautréamont and Antonin Artaud). Kristeva has also written of Jackson Pollock and his relation to the *chora*.[14]

Depressing? Rothko?

One of the clichés surrounding Mark Rothko is that his art is (4) 'tragic' or 'depressing'. It seems to be gloomy, about 'tragic' subjects, it has 'a great tragic voice',[15] it employs sombre oxblood colours and blacks. Well, yes, this is Rothko's style. For a while the Tate Gallery in London sold a postcard in its gallery shop which showed a youth sitting alone in the grey Rothko Room, looking dejected. This was a cliché: one went into the Rothko Room, *maaan*, to feel real sad, *maaan*. To crown this view, critics pointed out that Rothko committed suicide. Not in his youth, nor like Vincent van Gogh, in the midst of his life, but aged sixty-seven, in 1970. As so often, Rothko's suicide is seen as an ultimate gesture, the ultimate romantic act of an intensely romantic artist. The suicide changes the critical perception of Rothko's art, and 'explains' the austere later mural series and the single colour paintings of the late 1960s. Rothko's suicide enables critics to say, *ah ha*, so those grey and black paintings *were* about something tragic and religious. As with Jackson Pollock, Rothko's death is seen as the crowning point of an artistic life. What a heroic way to go, shooting oneself in a New York studio.

This view of Mark Rothko as the heroic rebel is taken up by British poet Jeremy Reed in *Lipstick, Sex and Poetry*:

> We may not create our best works until later in life, but they must come about as a consequence of the revolution against conformity. We have to go against our selves in order to find the way forward, break what we had once in order to rebuild it. I am with the continuous protest that calls for the re-evaluation of truth. The great poets of this century, Rilke, Yeats, Lowell, all undid their early work and rebuilt it. The figurative painter grows into the abstract expressionist, then develops to the interior resonance of a Rothko, then breaks it all up to integrate the respective components into something new [16]

For some art critics, Mark Rothko was asking too much of abstraction, or of colour. He was asking colour to carry too much of his meaning. Giles Auty wrote:

> By eliminating and relying entirely on soft, amorphous forms to do his latter artistic bidding, Rothko placed great and possibly unbearable strain on colour. Indeed colour became his sole vehicle for distinguishing different forms of content. [17]

III

THE AMERICAN RENAISSANCE: MARK ROTHKO AND ABSTRACT EXPRESSIONISM

Rothko's mixture resulted in a series of glowing color structures that have no exact parallel in modern art... if Rothko had not existed, we would not even know of certain color possibilities in modern art. This is a technical accomplishment of magnitude. But Rothko's real genius was that out of color he had created a language of feeling.

Robert Motherwell[1]

The art historical aspects of Abstract Expressionism have been discussed in detail elsewhere, in countless places. One knows how the great 'renaissance' of American postwar art grew out of European modernism, as many of the artists in war-torn Europe fled to America, New York City often being their first port of call (Piet Mondrian, Jacques Lipchitz, Fernand Léger, André Masson, Yves Tanguy, Salvador Dali, Max Ernst and Marc Chagall came to New York, among many others). One knows, too, that American postwar art, and in particular the New York School, enshrined subject matter, heroic gestures, the Surrealist unconscious and a distinctly apolitical stance. Despite being abstract, Abstract Expressionist painters were very concerned with subject matter. Barnett Newman affirmed the primacy of subject matter. The issue, he said, for painters such as himself, Adolph Gottlieb, Jackson Pollock and others, was not about formalism, technique, surface and so on, but: 'what are we going to paint?'[2]

One knows about the enormous debt that Abstract Expressionism had to Russian Constructivism, to the Dadaists and Surrealists, to Italian futurism, to Fauvism, to Cubism, to Mondrian's abstractions (Mondrian's post-Platonic ascetic geometric abstraction), and so on. What is clear, too, is that no amount of traditional or art historical talk of 'influences' and cross-fertilization and exchange of ideas can explain away the majesty of the art of Jackson Pollock, Barnett Newman, Clyfford Still, Franz Kline, Robert Motherwell and Willem de Kooning. Abstract Expressionism was not simply another re-hashing of European modernist gestures and philosophies, it was a distinct breakthrough or progression. One cannot look at the enormous canvases with their great splotches of colour and not admit that something different was happening in New York in the 1940s and 1950s. True, one could point out Cubism, or look back to the broken colour of the Impressionists.

Somehow, that sort of talk diminishes a work, takes away its fire, as if, well, it's all happened before, or, well, the seeds of it were sown decades ago, which somehow renders the new work null and void. One might as well state that Leonardo da Vinci, probably the world's greatest artist, simply drew on traditions and norms formed in the Quattrocento and Trecento by Fra Angelico, Piero della Francesca, Giotto and Masaccio. Of course Leonardo used these existing formats and ideas. But he made something new with them – something quite extraordinary too. For, although one talks of Mark Rothko's canvases containing 'mystery' and 'transcendence', Leonardo had evoked greater mysteries and deeper transcendence in paintings such as *The Virgin Mary and Child with St Anne* (1508, Louvre). And, in

Pompeii the wall paintings, which so impressed Rothko, had also done the Rothko thing two thousands years before Rothko. One can go back further, to Lascaux and prehistoric cave paintings...

Mark Rothko can be seen as part of the movement or ideology of High Modernism, which Fredric Jameson defined as the world that had to be overthrown in the postmodernist era:

> Abstract Expressionism, the great modernist poetry of Pound, Eliot or Wallace Stevens; the International Style (Le Corbusier, Frank Lloyd Wright, Mies); Stravinsky; Joyce, Proust, Mann...[3]

One strain of Abstract Expressionism was grandiose – it has been called the 'Abstract Sublime'. It is in the works of Barnett Newman, Mark Rothko, Franz Kline and Clyfford Still that the tenets of High Modernism were taken to their extreme. Abstract Expressionism exalted exaltation itself, the heroic, phallic thrust into the Existential void. It was this high octane emotionalism which scared off later painters such as arch Minimalist (and late 'maximalist') Frank Stella. In *Working Space*, Stella writes:

> My dream, or perhaps my desire, as far as painting went, has already been realized to a certain extent by postwar abstract expressionism, especially by Pollock and de Kooning, but I sensed something in their work which worried me more than the stunning level of their accomplishment impressed me. I sensed a hesitancy, a doubt of some vague dimension which made their work touching, but to me somehow too vulnerable. (158)

The two key painters of the 'Abstract Sublime' were Barnett Newman and Mark Rothko. Barnett Newman was a canny theoretician,[4] as his writings demonstrate. While Clyfford Still despised the authority of tradition,[5] Newman and Rothko revelled in it. While Newman and others denied the rhetoric of exultation in their theoretical writings, their paintings shouted it. Newman's canvases usually had religious, symbolic, metaphysical or cosmic titles and projects: there were paintings of creation, singularity, totality and unity: the *Onement* series, *Day Before One* (Kunstmuseum, Basle), *The Beginning* (Chicago), *Day One* (Whitney Museum), the *Be* series (*Be I*, Detroit); many paintings were concerned with a cosmic light: *Primordial Light* (Houston), *Anna's Light* (1968, Kawamura Memorial Museum of Art, Japan), *Black Fire* (Philadelphia), *Noon-Light* (Houston), *White Fire* (Kunstmuseum, Basel), *Voice of Fire* (Ottawa); other works referred to Biblical, Judæo-Christian and Creation/ *Genesis* themes: *The Word, Abraham* (MOMA, New York), *The Stations of the Cross* (Washington), *Jericho* (Paris), *Covenant* (Washington), *Cathedra* (Amsterdam), *Chartres* (private collection), and the *Canto* lithographs (Fogg Art Museum); there were also paintings that referred to mythic or religious personalities: *Vir Heroicus Sublimis* (MOMA, New York), *The Queen of the Night* (Osaka, Japan), *Joshua* (Chicago), *Adam* (Tate Modern, London), *Dionysius* (Washington), *Ulysses* (Houston), *Uriel* (private collection) and *Achilles* (Washington).

Barnett Newman's paintings emphasized verticality, frontality, flatness, single-colour, all-overness, unified space, and grand scale. Newman developed his first stripe/ zip paintings in the late 1940s: *Onement I* (1948, MOMA, New York) was the breakthrough painting: it was not a conscious, deliberate decision, Newman said, to make the stripe: it happened. What he was doing, he said, was 'emptying the canvas by assuming the thing empty, and suddenly in this particular painting, *Onement*, I realized that I had filled the surface' (E. De Antonio, 67).

The formal invention, the 'zip', divides immense horizontal areas of colour. Sometimes Barnett Newman's 'zip' is meticulously painted, with smooth, unbroken edges, as in *Who's Afraid of Red, Yellow and Blue II* (1967, Stuttgart) and *Now I* (Madrid). At other times it is distinctly ragged and unpolished, as in *Right Here* (1954, Amsterdam) and *The Promise* (1949, New York), in which two white 'zips', one smooth and one rough, stand side by side in an area of black. In some paintings (*Treble*, 1960, New York, and *The Stations of the Cross*), the Newman 'zip' is defined 'negatively', by the brushmarks on each side of the stripe, which is left blank: it is defined by an absence. In *Tertia* (1964, Stockholm) and *The Third* (1962, Walker Art Center), the orange background to the left of the yellow stripe is left unpainted and ragged. Sometimes the large areas of colour are relatively uniform, as in *Onement no. 6* (1953, Wisman Family Collection), while in other paintings, such as *Cathedra* (1951, Stedelijk Museum, Amsterdam), the colour is broken up in lights and darks, though it never loses its sense of being a single colour.

In some paintings by Barnett Newman colour is applied meticulously and unbroken, as in *The Gate* (1954, Amsterdam) or *The Voice* (1950, MOMA, New York). Sometimes the fields of colour are deliberately mixed with darker tones – this often occurs in the blue canvases, where ultramarines mix with prussian blues: *Onement V* (1952, private collection), *L'Errance* (1953, New York), and *Ulysses* (1952, Houston). Newman's *Anna's Light* (1968, Kawamura Memorial Museum of Art, Japan) uses one of the most radiant reds in painting, like the equally incandescent red in Newman's *Vir Heroicus Sublimis*. The zip breaks up the areas of colour.

Barnett Newman considered his sense of drawing and planning an important part of his art. But it is the vastness of the areas of colour in Barnett Newman's paintings that is so striking. In *Vir Heroicus Sublimis* there are four stripes, which create five rectangles: the central rectangular area is by far the largest: the 'zips' are placed in the left- and right-hand thirds of the painting, as often in a Newman work. The central expanse of colour is what strikes one first in *Vir Heroicus Sublimis*, as in *Anna's Light*.

Barnett Newman affirmed the openness of his paintings. They were not so much about objects, or spaces, or graphic elements: they were open paintings (E. De Antonio, 159). In *Cathedra* the sense of carefully controlled architectonics is apparent: the whitish stripe is nearly central, dividing the painting into huge zones of blue: the off-centre geometry of the white stripe is balanced by the second, pale blue stripe on the right-hand side of the canvas. In *Anna's Light*, when the glow of the mid-red has softened and been absorbed by the viewer, one becomes aware of the sense of proportion and scale: there are two bands of white, one very thin band on the left hand edge, and a larger band on the right-hand edge.

In the *Who's Afraid of Red, Yellow and Blue* series of the mid/late 1960s, Barnett Newman showed that he could take colours as apparently simple and direct as the three primary colours and make them submit to his æsthetic project of metaphysical totality.[6] *Who's Afraid of Red, Yellow and Blue I* (1966, private collection) pushed the blue and yellow to the edges of the vertical format painting, so that the red was dominant. *Who's Afraid of Red, Yellow and Blue II* (1967, Stuttgart) again used red as the main ingredient: the blue and yellow were as before confined to narrow zips in the centre and edges of the composition. *Who's Afraid of Red, Yellow and Blue III* (1966-67, Stedelijk Museum, Amsterdam) took the colour format of the first *Who's Afraid of Red, Yellow and Blue*, and applied it to one of Newman's distinctive vast horizontal paintings. The immense expanse of scarlet recalls *Vir Heroicus Sublimis* and *Anna's Light*. *Who's Afraid of Red, Yellow and Blue IV* (1969-70, Berlin) squashed the dark blue in between two enormous planes of red and yellow.

Despite his fierce anti-art bias, Clyfford Still was interested in the notion of the 'sublime'. Still's *1947-M* (private collection), like the works of Mark Rothko and Barnett Newman, exudes an aura of the 'Abstract Sublime'. The rippling curtains of paint in Still's

1947-M look forward to late Rothko and Morris Louis. Still's *1955-D* (Marisa del Re Gallery, New York) is a large (117 inch) near-square of deep, sonorous red. Like Barnett Newman's all-over canvases, Still's *1955-D* seems an assertive, 'uncompromising' painting at first. It does not seem to give much of itself away. It seems enclosed, caught up in itself. It is one huge red square, an exploded version of Kasimir Malevich's earlier, and much smaller, red squares. Yet Still's painting, the closer one looks, reveals itself to be a lyrical meditation upon pure colour, in the manner of Rothko's beloved Henri Matisse.

For Helen Frankenthaler, colour was the prime æsthetic foundation. Frankenthaler's liquescent stains, such as in *Santorini* (Chicago), contain none of the existential angst that characterized much of Abstract Expressionist painting. Frankenthaler managed to continue making Abstract Expressionist paintings long after the heyday was over (indeed, right up to the 2000s).

Robert Motherwell spoke of painting in terms of music, which chimes with Mark Rothko's own post-Nietzschean theory of painting. The marks Motherwell made in his paintings recalled, he said, the polyphonic patterns of music – African, Oriental and mediæval music. Motherwell was also an advocate, like many postwar American artists, of Eastern mysticism. Motherwell's huge *Open Series* paintings evoked the Zen Buddhist void, mixing large areas of single colour with patches of calligraphic marks in the Oriental manner. While Franz Kline did not acknowledge Oriental calligraphy as a direct influence on his heavily gestural canvases, Motherwell was happy to point out this or that influence.

THE PATRIARCHAL SLANT OF MARK ROTHKO
AND ABSTRACT EXPRESSIONISM

Mark Rothko's art is patriarchal, masculine art. Or it comes out of the patriarchal, masculine world of Abstract Expressionism. The actual paintings of the 1950s and 1960s are full of vague, vaporous, floating, liquid masses of colour, aspects of formalism which seem to look towards the 'feminine'. That is, Rothko's clouds and smudged rectangles seem to be 'feminized' visions of abstraction. They are not hard and harsh marks on canvas. They are mutable, absorbing, flowing, the aspects associated in mainstream patriarchy with the 'feminine'. Of course, these are foolishly simplistic notions, but they are the sort of symbolic associations that are made in art criticism in reference to painters such as Rothko.

The world of the Abstract Expressionists was distinctly masculine and patriarchal: one sees this in the 'heroic' acts of creation, the bombastic gestures, such as Jackson Pollock aggressively stretching and dripping on his canvases on the floor, enshrined in the famous black and white photographs (by Hans Namuth); there was the sheer size of the Abstract Expressionists' canvases, so large they had to be painted on the floor, or by standing on ladders. There had been large paintings before – Michelangelo's Sistine Chapel, for example – but (nearly) every Abstract Expressionist painting was massive. Nearly every painting was eight or nine feet tall and the same or more wide. Barnett Newman's *Vir Heroicus Sublimis*, one of the *meisterwerks* of the Abstract Expressionist era, was over seventeen feet wide, as was *Who's Afraid of Red, Yellow and Blue III* and *Uriel*. Newman's *Who's Afraid of Red, Yellow and Blue IV* and *Anna's Light* were twenty feet across.

The effect of the more excessive side of Abstract Expressionism was a grandiose form of art which, coupled with the soaring religious themes, reminded one at times of the pompous gestures of political art – most insidiously, the ideological bombast of the

Nazi stadium rallies. This is a controversial allusion, for Mark Rothko and his cronies had lived through the Second World War, and Rothko was conscious of his Jewish heritage. Yet, the more 'sublime' reaches of Abstract Expressionism do have this melodramatic, operatic quality. It seems to be reaching for something it is not equipped either to grasp or to put to use. It is an art of striving or Nietzschean 'becoming', and this journey towards transcendence sometimes produces paintings that are so self-consciously 'sublime', 'epic' and 'heroic' that they fall into bathos or fascism. This is rare, however, and much of the 'Abstract Sublime' painting (by Motherwell, Newman, Still, Kline and Rothko) is rigorously, sensuously good art.

MARK ROTHKO AND CORNWALL

Mark Rothko came over to England in 1958 and stayed at Little Parc Owles, with the Cornish artist Peter Lanyon and his family. Rothko was looking for a suitable chapel which he could decorate. Rothko met some of the St Ives luminaries, such as Patrick Heron. To Linden Travers, the wife of James Holman, chairman of a local engineering firm, Rothko said 'painting is such agony'. Peter Fuller writes in his essay "St Ives" of Lanyon, regarded as one of Britain's best postwar abstract artists:

> Lanyon was also developing a reputation in New York. He got to know Mark Rothko well and brought the American over to St Ives in 1958... We need not be surprised if Lanyon, the figurative painter of the vanishing field, finds a soul mate in Rothko, the great abstract painter of the absent figure. Both were struggling for that 'Higher Symbolism' in painting, and both, in different ways, were aware of its virtual impossibility – of the risk of losing everything, including themselves, in the void of sensation and 'pure' abstraction. (ib., 110)

The Cornish seaside town of St Ives has a special place in British art history. Taken together, in one broad sweep, the number of talented artists who worked in St Ives at one time or another is quite extraordinary, considering the tiny scale of the place. St Ives is the site – the whole town is a studio space – of a host of celebrated figures in British art: Barbara Hepworth, Ben Nicholson, Patrick Heron, Francis Bacon, Bernard Leach, Naum Gabo, Alfred Wallis, Terry Frost, Lanyon, Adrian Stokes, Wilhelmina Barns-Graham, David Bomberg, Alan Davie, Roger Hilton, Bryan Wynter and Breon O'Casey. The roll-call of distinguished visitors to St Ives included Victor Pasmore, Laura Knight, and Rothko's fellow New Yorkers, Helen Frankenthaler, Mark Tobey and Larry Rivers.

It is odd to think of the big names of the art world descending on the sleepy Cornish harbour town. Somehow, the words New York City, Abstract Expressionism and provincial St Ives seem incongruous. Yet, when one looks closer at the St Ives art scene, one sees an enormous love of landscape, symbolism, the *avant garde*, Surrealism and, importantly, abstraction. Painters such as Patrick Heron, Peter Lanyon, Alan Davie, Wilhelmina Barns-Graham and Terry Frost were clearly influenced by American postwar art.

The surrounding landscape of West Penwith is deeply influential on St Ives painting. The moors, the purple heather, the windswept beaches, the menhirs and stone circles, the little cottages, the disused mineshafts. Mark Rothko would have been sympathetic to this landscape, and to the landscape painting tradition, for it was very often abstract. This Cornish part of the planet is a world away from the grime and noise and skyscraper canyons of Gotham City. It's understandable that an artist who seeks solitude like Rothko should come to St Ives. The wonderful studios of St Ives – one of the main attractions of the place – are a world away from the vast, high-ceilinged, white-washed lofts and studios of New York City.

One can still wander into some of the Porthmeor Studios, and they are still magical spaces. In New York studios one looks out onto a grid of busy streets, yellow taxis, fire escapes, giant billboards in and around Broadway and 42nd Street, Union Square, the Village and the Bowery. In St Ives, the sea dominates the windows of the studios which overlook the beach. The sea is always there – it appears in many of the St Ives artists' works. The abstract landscape tradition in painting, which chimes so much with Rothko, Newman, Motherwell, Louis and Still, is still going strong in Cornwall. One only has to visit contemporary galleries such as Salthouse Gallery, the excellent Penwith Gallery, Rainydays Gallery in Penzance and Newlyn Art Gallery, to see that the influence of Rothko and Abstract Expressionism is alive and well (as well as the influence of Impressionism, Expressionism, J.M.W. Turner, John Sell Cotman, and British landscapists).

It is significant that Mark Rothko has been regarded as much more important by art critics around the world than almost any of the St Ives artists (Peter Lanyon, Patrick Heron, Terry Frost, Anke Petersen, Ben Nicholson, John Wells, Roger Hilton, Breon O'Casey and Anthony Benjamin). But then, very few postwar British artists have achieved the kind of fame Rothko, Jasper Johns, Andy Warhol and Willem de Kooning have (one thinks of David Hockney, Peter Blake, Francis Bacon and R.B. Kitaj). Furthermore, there isn't an abstract painter in 20th century Britain who has been as widely celebrated as Rothko.

For Patrick Heron, when they manipulate colour, painters are shaping the 'very stuff of which sight or vision consists'. For Heron, colour and space are part of a continuum; space and colour become interchangeable. In 1969 he wrote:

Because painting is exclusively concerned with the seen, as distinct from the known, pictorial space and pictorial colour are virtually synonymous.[7]

For Patrick Heron, painting must move towards an all-over

sensation of colour: painting, he wrote, should 'end in pure sensation of colour'.[8] One thinks of post-painterly abstraction, in particular the 'pure colour' of Mark Rothko and Morris Louis.

Peter Fuller, in his grumpy, eccentric way, reckoned that the New York School did not 'influence' British painters in a one-way flow of æsthetic information. After 1958, Fuller said, American painting no longer triumphed over the rest the world.[9] Fuller thought that Patrick Heron influenced the American painters: 'I believe not only that Heron's stripe paintings preceded those of Morris Louis, but also that they are better, much better, in æsthetic terms'.[10] Compared with Patrick Heron's late Fifties work, Fuller claims, 'there is a dowdy and depressing feel about even the best Morris Louis canvases. With few exceptions, Louis's paintings, today, have the look of last season's used and abused fashions' (ib., 218). Fuller's negative appraisal of Morris Louis is part of his basic anti-American, pro-British philosophy. Instead of spending idiot amounts of money on Louis's canvases, Fuller said, collectors would be better off buying Patrick Herons. In fact, it appears the other way around now: Heron's art is far more 'provincial' and 'dowdy' than Louis's.

Peter Fuller may be right about the influence of Patrick Heron on Morris Louis, with regard to the coloured stripe motif of the latter. But Patrick Heron's own stripe paintings – the stripes moving horizontally across a portrait format canvas – look suspiciously like Mark Rothko's late 1940s and early 1950s paintings. Rothko's paintings of the late 1940s, such as *Number 11* (1949, Washington) and *Number 17* (1947, New York), are clearly the ancestors of Patrick Heron's late 1950s paintings (such as the Tate's *Horizontal Stripe Painting*). Heron acknowledged the American painters many times. The 1956 Abstract Expressionist show at the Tate Gallery deeply affected Heron's work.

There are many similarities between Patrick Heron and Mark Rothko, the closer one looks. Both artists greatly admired Henri Matisse, and the Matissean dedication to the power of pure colour. Both painters cited Matisse's *Red Studio* as an especially poignant work. Later, Heron reacted against the influence of the American abstractionists.

For Mark Rothko, *Red Studio,* in the Museum of Modern Art in New York, was a painting he associated with his birth as a painter: 'from those months and that looking every day all of my painting was born', he said of the hours he'd spent looking at Matisse's painting. The affinities between the floating objects in Matisse's painting and Rothko's work are obvious: in both painters the 'things' or forms are overwhelmed by the radiance of the colour.[11]

IV

MARK ROTHKO'S ÆSTHETICS

A man who as a physical being is always turned toward the outside, thinking that his happiness lies outside him, finally turns inward and discovers that the source is within him.

Søren Kierkegaard

Mark Rothko's æsthetics were largely drawn from the classics of European culture (Rothko was Russian, and came to the New World when he was ten, in 1913). For example, Rothko admired Friedrich Nietzsche, and his art can interpreted as a post-Nietzschean art (Dionysian rather than Apollonian (R. Hobbs, 1972), as out of Nietzsche's *Birth of Tragedy*, 1872). Every intellectual and writer seems to have to grapple with Friedrich Nietzsche as some time or other (especially the French philosophers: Georges Bataille, Hélène Cixous, Sarah Kofman, Gilles Deleuze, Luce Irigaray, Jacques Derrida, and Jean-Paul Sartre). One of Nietzsche's many intriguing phrases or maxims was that 'the sense of the tragic increases and declines with sensuousness' (1923, 98). The more tragic art becomes, the more sensuous too. It is an argument that is borne out by a study of drama – think of the highly erotic quality of William

Shakespeare's tragedies, a built-in eroticism which contemporary performers do not need to do much to enhance. And it is true that Rothko's canvases do become more sensual the more tragic they are.[1]

The Existentialists and 'tragic' philosophers and writers of Europe were also admired by the Abstract Expressionists (Søren Kierkegaard, Fyodor Dostoievsky, Franz Kafka, Jean-Paul Sartre, Albert Camus, Maurice Merleau-Ponty). Mark Rothko saw himself very much in the vein of Dostoievsky, Kierkegaard, Nietzsche and Stéphane Mallarmé. He quoted philosophers such as Kirkegaard in his lectures (Kirkegaard is perfect for Rothko: this is typical of Kirkegaard's philosophy: 'Anxiety is the dizziness of freedom'. Rothko was creating art in the mid-century era, when the French Existentialists and writers (such as Sartre, André Gide and Camus) were enshrining Germanic and Scandinavian philosophers such as Nietzsche and Kirkegaard. Nothing in Rothko's art startles if one recalls that an atomic bomb or two had been dropped on Japan and the truth of the concentration camps was becoming apparent to the rest of the world. This was an era of a Cold War, Senator MacCarthy and Left Bank philosophers who wrote gargantuan tomes entitled *Being and Nothingness*. Rothko knew that life could be horrible. Or, rather, that people could be horrible. Hence the seriousness of his art.[2] Natural that he should admire writers such as the Greek dramatist Aeschylus. The Greek tragedy view of the world accords well with Rothko's worldview, though he later came to prefer William Shakespeare.

What Mark Rothko liked about Shakespeare was his all-encompassing vision of life: Shakespeare, Rothko felt, embraced all aspects and feelings in life.[3] Which is true, for in few other artists is there such a broad vision of the world and human life. And not only a comprehensive worldview, Shakespeare is also tender and compassionate (in *King Lear*, *Hamlet* and *The Tempest*, the three plays which come immediately to mind in connection with Mark Rothko). Rothko would later appreciate the importance of irony in his sense of tragedy. Irony is a way of defending oneself against the slings and arrows etc etc.

In his notes for a lecture at the Pratt Institute, Mark Rothko listed some points which are a broad outline of his own art:

A clear preoccupation with death
Sensuality
Tension
Irony
Wit, humor
A few grains of the ephemeral, a chance
About 10 per cent of hope (1958)

One can usefully apply these tenets to Mark Rothko's art: one sees that the critical machinery has tended to exalt the considerations of death and the sensuality in Rothko's art, and to suppress irony, wit, humour, chance and the ephemeral. The elements of wit and irony and humour in the traditional view of Rothko do not square with the vision of Rothko as a troubled, tragic painter. Yet any survey of Rothko's *œuvre* would reveal that Rothko was not being solemnly tragic and transcendent all the time, or even for most of the time. The first three prescriptions – death, sensuality and tension – are modulated by the next three: irony, wit/ humour and chance. Of course, in the literary reading of tragedy as a form, irony is an important ingredient – or at least, it is in interpretations of tragic form from Friedrich Nietzsche onwards.

Mark Rothko's cloud-like shapes were not mere blobs of paint, they were definitely things or objects, or feelings, something graspable, perhaps organic or biomorphic forms: 'the shapes in the pictures are the performers', he commented (1947-48). 'My new areas of color are things' (in W. Seitz). Each shape was individual, set in its own context. The forms, Rothko said, were simultaneously non-representational and figurative, they were not specific to this or that situation or individual, but nevertheless referred to human experience. The shapes, Rothko said, 'have no direct association with any particular visible experience, but in

them one recognizes the principle and passion of organisms'
(1947-48).

Mark Rothko's paintings are often, as with Jackson Pollock, entitled *Number X*, or they have titles referring to their colours: *White and Green in Blue* and *Grayed Olive Green, Red on Maroon*, and he used the ubiquitous 20th century title for an artwork, *Untitled*. The use of the title *Untitled*, which occurred with Rothko's radical transformation of his art in the late 1940s, was not wholly satisfactory for him. Each work is clearly a personality or special object in its own right, so one sees Rothko beginning to label his paintings with colours, which personalizes the work.

The titles which are simply numbers do not describe the content of the painting in any way. They are simply numerical marks, a reference system for the artist. The titles which are colours are also similarly ambiguous and vague. One can see for oneself if a painting is 'greyed olive green', 'red on maroon', or 'white and green in blue'. Yes, one can see the white and green colours in the surrounding blue colour. The title does nothing to promote understanding of the painting. Unless, perhaps, it really *is* about pure colour, and nothing else. This is not so with Mark Rothko's art, however. His paintings are always more than simply fields or realms of colour. Jasper Johns entitled his creations *Target* or *Flag*, but clearly there was a lot more going on than was suggested by the title. It's the same with Rothko: his titles *White and Green in Blue* or *White Stripe* are featherweight indications of the huge canvases, tiny, vague indicators of the monumentality of the paintings.

Mark Rothko had a religious view of art-making. For him the moment of creation was miraculous.

The most important tool the artist fashions through constant practice is faith in his ability to produce miracles when they are needed. Pictures must be miraculous... (1947-48)

Faith. Belief. Or as Søren Kirekgaard put it:

> If I am capable of grasping God objectively, I do not believe, but precisely because I cannot do this I must believe.

At the moment of creation, art can be miraculous, Mark Rothko said: but later, the artist was as distanced from his creation as the viewer: the aim was to instigate that initial revelation again (1947-48).

Adolph Gottlieb wrote most of the oft-cited letter to the *New York Times*, with its calls for an imaginative, mythic, large, adventurous and abstract art. The only sentence that Mark Rothko apparently wrote in that oft-quoted letter was: 'only that subject matter is valid which is tragic and timeless' (1943).

One can see the imprint of Mark Rothko in these words, which certainly do apply to Rothko's art. Despite being abstract, Rothko view of art was humanist and firmly centred in human experience. He spoke continually of human 'dramas' ('I think of my pictures as dramas' [1947-48]), of Greek tragedy as a model or parallel for his conception of the human, existential drama of being alive. It is the human figure that is at the centre of Rothko's art, as it was for the German Expressionists (Max Beckmann, Ernst Ludwig Kirchner, Emil Nolde) or the Italian Renaissance painters.

In "The Portrait and the Modern Art" Mark Rothko argued for an art based on the human figure, on its character, emotions and drama. It wasn't so much any one particular human individual that Rothko was interested in portraying, but an ideal or general expression of humanity. It was the essence of a tragic, existential experience that Rothko was after, as embodied in the human figure. It is interesting that Rothko speaks of feeling reluctant to leave the human figure, because it could not work for him.[4] He moved into a wide-ranging, even universal view of humanity, so that the 'whole of man's experience becomes his [the artist's] model' (1958). He had to abandon the figure, but the sense of humanity and human existential passion persisted throughout his work, so that his forms and paintings can be seen in equivalent terms for human, figurative emotions.

In this sense, Mark Rothko did not see his work as 'abstract'.[4] The term implied a distantiation from reality which was not Rothko's programme. Like Constantin Brancusi, terms such as 'abstraction' did not apply to him: his work is more correctly realist or expressionist in the sense that it aims to get at some reality or expression which is firmly rooted in the world and in people.

The departure from representation, Adolph Gottlieb and Mark Rothko asserted, was simply a different way of approaching a subject, the aim being not to dilute but to intensify the subject (1943). 'Abstract' meant something cool, detached, indifferent, mathematical, uninvolved, whereas Rothko saw his art as very much embroiled in life and emotions. Rather than being detached from the world, Rothko maintained that he was immersed in it, in the materiality of it (1945). Instead of distance, detachment and non-involvement, Rothko's aim was always to create an intimate and profound relationship between painting and viewer. Hence the large scale, the project to immerse and absorb the viewer, so that an intimacy is created between painting and viewer. Critic Lucy Lippard wrote of scale:

Most discussions of scale consider it a strictly optical experience... But a sense of scale is also a *sense* proper. Scale is *felt* and cannot be communicated either by photographic reproduction or by description.[5]

Mark Rothko wrote of his intentions with regard to scale thus:

I paint very large pictures... The reason I paint them... is precisely because I want to be very intimate and human. To paint a small picture is to place yourself outside your experience, to look upon an experience as a stereopticon view or with a reducing glass. However you paint the larger picture, you are in it. It isn't something you command. (1951)

Mark Rothko's view is wholly accurate, but some of the largest and most monumental paintings are tiny: some of the Early

Netherlandish masters, for example, such as Petrus Christus, Jan van Eyck and Geertgen tot Sin Jans, produced very small panels which contained whole worlds which were just as consuming and vital as the largest of Abstract Expressionist canvases. But applied to his own paintings, Rothko's statement reveals again his goal of absorption and immersion. The aim was to produce a totality of viewing experience, where the painting works quietly but forcefully towards consuming the viewer wholly. The viewer loses her/ his separate identity, and is intended to merge with the painting.[6] In Rothko's statements, such as in this one from *Tiger's Eye* (1949), one sees Rothko's struggle to achieve a total commun-ication between the art object and the viewer:

> The progression of a painter's work, as it travels in time from point to point, will be toward clarity, toward the elimination of all obstacles between the painter and the idea, and between the idea and the observer. (1949)

Mark Rothko cared greatly about the way his paintings were perceived by the public. He was very sensitive to the way his paintings were assessed by critics, at times wishing that nothing would be said about them. It was the viewer's direct experience of the artwork that counted for him. This was sacred: the painting-viewer relationship. The conditions of the gallery had to be just right. In a set of instructions sent to the Whitechapel Galery in London for his 1961 show there, Rothko made some suggestions about hanging conditions. The walls, Rothko offered, should be 'considerably off-white with umber and warmed by a little red'. Rothko's comments on lighting are interesting, and one can see how they have been incorporated by exhibitors of Rothko's works at subsequent shows:

> The light, whether natural or artificial, should not be too strong: the pictures have their own inner light and if there is too much light, the color in the picture is washed out and a distortion of their look occurs. The ideal situation would be to hang them in a normally lit room – that is the way they were painted. They should not be over-lit or

romanticized by spots; this results in a distortion of their meaning. They should either be lighted from a great distance or indirectly by casting lights at the ceiling or the floor. Above all, the entire picture should be evenly lighted and not strongly. (1961)

What's clear from this matter-of-fact explication of gallery lighting is how crucial things such as lighting and wall colour are – considerations that the viewer might take for granted. After all, everything is decided and in place by the time the gallery visitor enters the space. What the visitor does not know about are the hours of preparation and effort that have gone into making the gallery space exactly right. Some painters, and Mark Rothko was definitely one of this sort of artist, are acutely aware of gallery lighting, positioning, height above the floor, the colour of the walls, the order or sequence of the works, and so on. For the installation of his room of paintings at the Tate Gallery in London, Rothko sent a sample of the colour of his studio walls, in order to correlate the conditions on both sides of the Atlantic.

V

MARK ROTHKO'S MULTIFORM PAINTINGS OF THE 1940s-1960s

EARLY WORKS

It's worth looking at some of Mark Rothko's early works briefly: the figurative paintings of the mid- and late 1930s recall artists such as Pablo Picasso, Henri Matisse and German Expressionists such as Ernest Ludwig Kirchner, Max Beckmann, Emil Nolde and Karl Schmidt-Rottluff. The tendency is for blurred shapes, often with the distinctive black outline of German Expressionism around each form. The early works, many of them entitled *Untitled*, such as the full-length female nude in *Untitled* (1930, private collection) or a group of bathers (*Untitled*, late 1920s, Estate of Mark Rothko), clearly derive some of their inspiration from the art of Kirchner, Schmidt-Rottluff, Alexei von Jawlensky, Otto Mueller and Beckmann.

There is little, in these early 1930s paintings, that suggests the grandeur and rigorous abstraction of Mark Rothko's later works. Rothko paintings of the mid-1930s, such as *Woman Sewing*, or the

1932 *Interior* (both Washington), are essentially essays in restrained, flat, broken colour. The lack of volumetric, 3-D illusive space suggests Rothko's later abstractions, but if Rothko had stopped painting with these works, he would remain relatively unknown.

There is not much truly distinctive about these early figurative works. They achieve their power partly from the viewer knowing they are by Mark Rothko, and from the strength of the later works. Before 1936 Rothko painted a *Crucifixion* (whereabouts unknown) which draws heavily on the religious paintings of Emil Nolde, Max Beckmann and Lovis Corinth. These Expressionists in turn looked back to painters such as Albrecht Dürer, Martin Schöengauer, Hans Baldung and Matthias Grünewald with his immensely moving *Isenheim Altarpiece*. Rothko's Christ, though, is nowhere near as impassioned as Corinth's *Red Christ*, for example, or the Christs in Nolde's *Last Supper*, Beckmann's *Deposition* or Schmidt-Rottluff's woodcuts.

In the late 1930s and 1940s the influence of Surrealism (and Milton Avery) became more and more apparent. One sees the influence of Piet Mondrian in the flat, rectangular forms of *Subway Scene* (1941, Estate of Mark Rothko), while Joan Miró, André Masson, Max Ernst and Pablo Picasso are very much in evidence in the early 1940s paintings (in *Untitled*, *c.* 1944, Metropolitan Museum of Art, *Untitled, c.* 1944, Philadelphia, and *Untitled*, 1944-46, Guggenheim).

In these paintings one detects the enshrinement of mythological themes and imagery which is found in the European painters (Picasso, Ernst), as well as the first generation of Abstract Expressionists (Jackson Pollock, Clyfford Still, Adolph Gottlieb). Rothko and Gottlieb, like most of the Abstract Expressionists, asserted the primal mystery of their art. They wrote: '[n]o possible set of notes can explain our paintings' (1943).

The use of myth in Mark Rothko's art was about striving towards an archaic, primal subject matter, about 'primeval and predatory passions' (1943). Myth was not about escape, fantasy, beauty or romance, but a primitive authenticity. The archaic myths and symbols expressed fundamental truths – a view found in much of High Modernism, from James Joyce's appropriation of the Ulysses myth and T.S. Eliot's reworking of myth in *The Wasteland* to the music of Igor Stravinsky, and the prints of Pablo Picasso or Emil Nolde's madly dancing mænads. Gleaned from Robert Briffault, J.J. Bachofen, J.G. Frazer, Mircea Eliade, Sigmund Freud, Otto Rank and C.G. Jung, mythic themes were central to High Modernism. Rothko was a passionate devotee of the tenets of High Modernism. Mythological paintings of the mid-40s include *Rites of Lilith* (1945, Estate of Mark Rothko), *The Syrian Bull* (1943, private collection), *Birth of Cephalopods* (1944, MOMA, New York), *The Omen of the Eagle* (1942, Washington), *Antigone* (1941, Washington) and *Tiresias* (1944, private collection). The mythological and Surrealist paintings were inspired by the dramas of the ancient world – *The Omen of the Eagle*, for example, derived its theme from Aeschylus.[1]

What is striking also about the mid-1940s Surrealist, biomorphic works is how weak their colouration is. So intently was the artist concentrating on the shapes, drawing, compositions and mythological components of the paintings, he seems to have neglected colour, which is so strange when one considers just how important colour was in the later canvases. In a quasi-Surrealist painting such as *Poised Elements* (1944, private collection) there is a pallid red across the bottom quarter of the frame, but the rest of the painting is in thin greys. In *Tiresias*, for example, which is one of the more colourful of the mythological paintings, the colours are even so very restrained for Mark Rothko. There are warm colours here – yellow and gold in particular – but the impression is not of richness but, as in (nearly) all the mythological works, of a restraint, even timidity.

Once Mark Rothko had drawn his semi-abstract shapes, he gave them only the vestiges of colour. It was as if he was assured of the power of mythic images, he did not feel it necessary to give them a bold treatment in terms of colour. Thus, compared to Pablo

Picasso, Jean Arp and Joan Miro, Rothko's mythological paintings are extremely restrained. In *Slow Swirl at the Edge of the Sea* (1944, Estate of Mary Alice Rothko) or *Untitled* (1945, Estate of Mark Rothko) the predominant colour is a off-white, modulated by bands of slightly darker greys and browns. Rothko's temperance in colouration is very marked: red and yellow are used with great reserve, touched in only at points in the composition. True, works such as *Gethsemane* (1945, private collection) and *Primeval Landscape* (1945, Estate of Mark Rothko) contain slightly deeper colours, but still with a light grey predominating. The transformation into the rectangular paintings of the late 1940s onwards is all the more radical when one considers not only the sense of abstraction but of colouration: in *Multiform* (1948, Estate of Mark Rothko), *Number 22* (1949, MOMA, New York), *Magenta, Black, Green on Orange* (1949, Estate of Mary Alice Rothko) and other paintings of the 1947-49 era,

As one surveys the trajectory of Mark Rothko's career, one sees the Miró-like forms and quasi-Surrealist calligraphy of the mid-1940s expanding and softening at the edges; so that, during the late 1940s, the movement into the familiar mature Rothko style of open rectangular floating forms was complete. *Number 18* (1948-49, Vassar College Art Gallery, Poughkeepsie), *Multiform* (1948, Estate of Mark Rothko), and *Number 15* (1948, Washington) are typical canvases of this transitional period.

THE MULTIFORMS AND RECTANGLES

Once Mark Rothko had established some structures and rules for his mature art, around 1949, he explored the possibilities that large oil on canvas paintings offered. Some of the paintings used a blanched palette, such as *Number 11* (1949, Washington), with cream and white painted over watery blue, to pull it back to a very light tone. In another painting from the same year, though, Rothko began to delve into large areas of black, like so many other American postwar painters. *Untitled* (1949, Metropolitan Museum) layers black or a very dark blue over reds, yellows and whites. One could extract from Rothko's *œuvre* a group of paintings which might support a reading of Rothko as a dark, tragic painter of dark, tragic paintings.[2] There are works such as the mural commissions, the maroon paintings of the late 1950s or the black and grey pieces from the late 1960s, which would support a gloomy, introspective reading of Rothko's art.

It's true, some of his painting are like this. From the middle period of the 1950s one finds works such as *Earth and Green* (1955, Museum Ludwig, Cologne), which is a sombre composition of three colours, an earthy dark brown rectangle above a larger dark viridian rectangle against a prussian blue background. The *Untitled* painting of 1953 (Washington) has a large dark blue rectangle dominating the painting, but it is capped by an expanse of lipstick pink. Max Kozloff remarked:

> The radiant colours at their best effect an 'ignition' that results from the impact of a fierce palette upon an aloof and fastidious temperament [which] flusters exhaustion and begins to hold the haunted spectator longer than he intended. (1961)

Rothko's light was likened to a Biblical opening of the heavens by another critic, a light of annunciation and revelation.[3]

The sombre interpretation of Mark Rothko is knocked away by a survey of the paintings from the 1950s onwards. There are many, many more brightly coloured paintings than dark, brooding ones. *Orange, Red and Red* (1962, Dallas Museum of Art), for example, is excessively hotly coloured, with an enormous rosy orange rectangle above a darker red rectangle, backed by red. These radiant reds did not cease with the darkening into maroon of the Houston, Harvard and Seagram mural series either: Rothko continued to employ incandescent crimsons up until his death. The reds persist through the 'depressed' black and grey period of the late Sixties: two works, both called *Untitled* (both in Washington), are supremely, unashamedly, victoriously *red*. Not only red, but *red on red*.

In canvas after canvas are found sonorous yellows above equally sonorous yellows (*Untitled*, 1952, Tate Modern); radiant orange rectangles rising above carmine pink forms (*Number 12*, 1951, private collection); brilliant lemon hues above oranges and below soft lilacs (*Number 7*, 1951, Sarah Campbell Blaffer Foundation); and buttercup yellow forms above wine red and grey over dark red (*Orange, Wine, Gray on Plum*, 1961, Estate of Mark Rothko). In *Number 16* (1958, Estate of Mary Alice Rothko), a large tangerine form is a solid base to a strip of white across the central zone and a drab light chocolate upper form.

The sheer abundance of incandescent colour of mid-period Mark Rothko is striking. There is a long series of paintings, for example, which are founded on the brightest, most positive colours of the spectrum – yellow and orange – often modulated by another hot colour, red: *Number 7* (noted above); *Untitled* (1954, Yale University Art Gallery, New Haven) is a mainly yellow canvas, with a rectangle of lilac layered over a deep orange rectangle; another *Untitled* (1954, Estate of Mark Rothko), echoes the format of the previous *Untitled*, but leaves the dark orange to shine on its own; the 1955 *Untitled* (Estate of Mark Rothko) divides two huge fields of corn yellow with a broad band of white; *Orange and Yellow* (1954, Albright-Knox Art Gallery, Buffalo), *Yellow and Gold* (1956, MOMA, New York) and *Untitled* (1956, Estate of Mark Rothko) are three of Rothko's most vibrant paintings: the predominant colour is orange, the phosphorescence which is emphasized by being paired not with a complimentary colour, but with yellow.

As with some of Vincent van Gogh's wheatfields and sunflowers, this combination of orange and yellow is really intense. One could anchor these paintings to a tragic interpretation if one wished: one could see them as the final conflagration before the final apocalypse. Alternatively, one could see these six by seven foot yellow and orange canvases as life-affirming statements.

COLOUR AND MUSIC

Sometimes Mark Rothko modulated his yellows and oranges with the more proper consituents of the traditional colour wheel of colour theory. *Yellow Blue on Orange,* for example (1955, Carnegie Museum of Art, Pittsburgh), anchors the upper realm of burnished yellowy-gold with a middle blue, a suitable complimentary colour (which's modulated itself by white under-painting on top of orange underpainting). A painting of 1953 such as *Green and Maroon* (Phillips Collection, Washington) is also traditional, setting two 'opposites' beside each other – green and dark red – on top of a background of the third primary colour, blue. *Green, Red, Blue* (1955, Milwaukee Art Museum) offers a similar pattern of the three primary colours.

In the rectangular paintings, as in the murals, there is no frame around the canvas. This is a common occurrence in 20th century art. It is a question of relating inner and outside spaces, of providing a continuity between gallery, personal and painted space. Mark Rothko did not 'frame' his paintings, he explained, because he wished to do away with the box-like space of traditional painting.

In our inheritance we have space, a box in which things are going on. In my work there is no box. I do not work with space. There is a form without the box, and possibly a more convincing kind of form.4

Some of Mark Rothko's paintings directly recall Barnett Newman's: Rothko's *White Stripe* (private collection), for instance, is a fat rectangle some two yards on each side. It is covered in red, as in Newman's *Vir Heroicus Sublimis* and *Who's Afraid of Red, Yellow and Blue III*. As with the Seagram paintings, there are slightly darker rectangular forms discernible in the red ground. Contrasting the excursions in deep crimson, however, is a very bright wide stripe placed, as so often in Newman's 'zip' paintings, just off-centre.

In paintings such as *White Stripe*, Mark Rothko's art appears very much concerned with musicality, with the formal considerations of counterpoint, repetition and harmony, and the intense abstraction and emotionalism of music and poetry. The allusion to musical theory is of course wholly in keeping with Rothko's 'tragic', Nietzschean, emotional form of art-making. Music was crucial to Rothko not simply for a background sound in the studio (he often played Wolfgang Amadeus Mozart, *Don Giovanni, The Magic Flute*, opera, Johann Sebastian Bach and string quartets while working), but as a primary means of expression.

The musical analogies in Mark Rothko's art chime with his interest in Mozart, classical music and opera, with Friedrich Nietzsche (*The Birth of Tragedy*), with Greek philosophy, with the links between music, poetry and the spirit, with hermeticism and occultism, with the idea of the visual aspects of painting having sensory equivalents. Poets and psychologists call this principle synæsthesia, where the five senses blend together, where each of the senses has an equivalence with the other through metaphor and image (the *colour* of scents, for example, or, in reference to Rothko's art, how particular colours *sound*). The cultural references for synæsthesia in poetry, literature and music include French poets Charles Baudelaire, Arthur Rimbaud (his 'alchemy of the word'), Stéphane Mallarmé and Paul Verlaine, late 19th century *fin-de-siècle* art and Symbolist art.

Mark Rothko knew all about the theory of colours – how strong red was, for instance. How blue is calming, orange enlivening, and so on. Colours have real, measurable physical effects on people. Looking at Rothko's canvases musically, one can see his coloured rectangular forms in terms of sounds. Rothko used colours structurally, to build up a set of forms and inter-relationships between the colours and the size and shape of the forms. The blocks of colour can be approached (literally, 'heard') as blocks of sound. Thus, in a painting such as *Number 61 (Brown, Blue, Brown On Blue)* (1953, Panza di Biumo, Milan), three large oblongs of colour are arranged in the usual Rothkoan horizontal slabs on a ground of blue. Above is the largest form, a dark brownish colour. At the bottom, ultramarine. In the middle, a much lighter blue, a pallid sky blue. The 'sounds' this painting creates are heavy, low-pitched sounds enclosing a higher, clearer sound, which is the middle band of turquoise. Rothko knows that darker colours make for lower, more sombre sounds or effects, and lighter, warmer colours are louder and higher. Sometimes, tone and colour combine to produce a very noisy painting, such as Rothko's *White Stripe*. In Barnett Newman's *Vir Heroicus Sublimis* the all-over red is a giant, bold colour, proud, self-assured, indomitable. In another heroically huge Abstract Expressionist painting, Robert Motherwell's *Summer Open with Mediterranean Blue* (1974), the vast areas of mid-blue are suitably calming, in contrast to the harsh colouration of Motherwell's series of *Spanish Elegies* (from 1948 onwards).

Sometimes Mark Rothko would work against the stereotypical reading of colour in his paintings. Sometimes, blue – traditionally 'passive' – becomes active, while reds recede into darkness. Significantly, Rothko used an abundance of red in his late paintings, in particular in the two important commissions, the Seagram and the Houston Chapel paintings and other murals series. In these paintings, red is allowed to bleed dry, so that it is definitely not the hot, proud scarlet of Barnett Newman's *Vir Heroicus Sublimis,* or Clyfford Still's *1955-D* (Marisa del Re Gallery, New York). Instead, Rothko's dark red, the thing one notices immediately in the Houston Chapel or Seagram paintings, is a colour that has withdrawn from the heat and passion of life. It is a red that merges into a dark purple, a colour which connotes the purple of Imperial Rome, the purple of priestly robes, a colour of political and church power. The dark crimson of the Rothko Chapel and the Rothko Room is difficult to pin down. It is a mixture of red, black, brown, orange and white. One can see many colours in it, but the overriding impression is of sombreness, weight, meditation, authority, depth and humility.

CLOUDS

In Mark Rothko's 1962 *Blue and Gray* (Frederick Weisman Family Collection; the title is self-explanatory) a giant rectangular whitish-grey form hovers above a deep ultramarine rectangle of colour. I've just written 'hovers'. What does that mean? Does the white-grey form really 'hover'? One can't help clinging to terms such as 'hover', 'float' and 'swim' in relation to Rothko's abstract paintings. It's because Rothko's forms are diaphanous, iridescent, vague, the edges continually blurred. They seem gaseous or fluid, always about to be transformed into something else. One speaks, too, of one form being 'above' another, as if they are related spatially and directly, even though Rothko does not state this. One keeps thinking of Rothko's forms as real ('illusory') objects deployed in a 'real' ('illusory') space. One form is described as 'on top' of another, or next to it, and so on, when these are areas of colour merely, not solid (or near solid) form. In short, we're still taking about Renaissance pictorial æsthetics – *all*

Western art, no matter how 'experimental' or *avant garde*, is still firmly grounded Renaissance space.

Perhaps because Mark Rothko titled one of his paintings *White Cloud* (1956, private collection), a floating narrow white rectangle over a voluminous crimson ground, or referred to clouds, I think of his forms at times as clouds. Other critics have also seen the cloud connection. Clouds float, they are gases and liquids, drifting cathedrals of ice. They are large, like Rothko's works, and they are primal, elemental manifestations of primal, elemental energies. Furthermore, clouds inhabit the peopleless realms of the sky, and the sky, as one knows, is the realm of transcendence *par excellence*. If you want a sudden, large, 'cosmic' vision, whether in poetry, religion, or in 'real life', look up at the clouds. Clouds are where alien spaceships appear (*Close Encounters of the Third Kind*), and God speaks from inside clouds (in thousands of Renaissance paintings). Deities are taken to Heaven on clouds (the Virgin Mary in Her Assumption). Yet clouds, while having many religious, theological, symbolic and elemental connotations, are also distinctly figureless, which must attract Rothko.

So, in referring to clouds, Rothko cleverly activates a sense of divinity but without being too specific. There are no faces in his clouds (even though people have for millennia seen shapes in clouds). The religious properties of clouds – and smoke – fit in with Rothko's goal of evoking the numinous but remaining vague.

Thus, the cloud-shape works well, because it can be read however one wishes to read it. The notion of the cloud implies a form resting above or in front of another form, which Mark Rothko's paintings generally portray: the lighter shape, tonally, sits in front of the darker tones. This is not always the case: a painting such as *Number 117* (1961, collection: Donald Blinken) has two dark shapes on top of a lighter red colour. Of course, writing 'on top' assumes that the rectangular forms, the key Rothko motif, is always in front of the background. Perhaps it is the other way around: perhaps the floating oblongs are behind the surrounding colour, and the oblongs become holes. Alternatively, the floating forms and the enclosing colour could be all on one spatial plane. There is no distinct separation, for instance, between the rectangular forms and the surrounding colour. The edges of the forms are blurred, so that the forms bleed into the surrounding colour, and vice versa. Each area in the Rothko painting is not severely marked off, as in the 'hard edge' painters (such as Kenneth Noland or Ellsworth Kelly). The movement from one area of colour to another is gradual. Sometimes Rothko deployed four or five different colour values at the edges of his forms, to ensure that the movement from the form to the ground in which it swims would be gradual. In the typical Rothko painting, each form is not a separate entity but is connected to the other forms and colours. This is very apparent in the late mural series, where patterns are repeated, and slightly changed, so that the viewer cannot help making connections.

Mark Rothko's forms are, as he said, individual forms, not repetitions, in the Serial art or Minimal art manner. The individuality of each cloud-shape is stressed, so that each painting, even though it often has an 'impersonal' title such as *Number 117*, is really a one-off, complete in itself.

Mark Rothko refined his colours as he explored the possibilities of the floating rectangles format. He was more successful when he limited his main colour pattern to two or three colours. In *Green and Maroon* (1953) and *Green, Red, Blue* (1955), for example, the two main colours, green and red, are allowed to dominate, while the blue background modulates them and anchors them. The mainly orange and yellow paintings, too, work best when the alternative colours are kept to a minimum. Always these colours are painted on top of slightly different hues, so they are never simply pure red or pure yellow on top of orange or blue. But Rothko was usually careful to keep the main colour free of interference from other colours. Thus, though his rectangular forms are broken by other colours coming up from underneath, or by being painted over, they still remain intact and unified as single-colour fields in their own right. Even when Rothko deliberately broke up the unity of a rectangular form by scratching or thinning away the topmost colour to reveal the underpainting, as in the blue form of *Untitled* (1955, Philadelphia), the dominion of the blue rectangle is retained.

A painting such as *Earth and Green* (1955, Museum Ludwig, Cologne) is powerful, too, because the two main colours are allowed sovereignty, the blue background remaining subservient. It is when Mark Rothko experiments with more than three main colours that things get complicated, and are more likely to fail. A canvas like *Violet, Black, Orange, Yellow on White and Red* (1949, Guggenheim) attests in its title to its complex structure. Violet, orange and yellow prevail here, but around them is white surrounded with a black strip across the centre. *Violet, Black, Orange, Yellow on White and Red* manages to stay this side of messy: it is trying to do too many things at once. The attempts at symmetry and proportion and harmony (two dark red vertical stripes, for example, are placed at each side of the upper violet rectangle), manage to stabilize what could be a chaotic collection of colours. While colours such as red and black and yellow have been a part of painting for hundreds of years, colours such as bright violet are seldom found in such great quantities before the 20th century (one reason is technology and economics, in producing an unusual pigment like lilac or violet): Rothko is successful in his attempt in *Violet, Black, Orange, Yellow on White and Red* to make such as large proportion of violet work: but it could so easily go wrong. The lilac in *Untitled* (1951, Estate of Mark Rothko), for example, misses the mark: the white on tan surround does not harmonize with the vast lilac upper form, while the red lower rectangle is of the same mid-tone, and fails to resolve the painting. The *Untitled* of 1949 (Allen M. Turner, Chicago), meanwhile, is messy: drab green over bright grass green for the upper rectangle; blue over cream and yellow for the lower form; around them an off-white surround, painted over red.

A number of Mark Rothko's rectangular paintings of the 1950s use as a major component one of the most difficult colours to control successfully: white. In *White, Red on Yellow* (1958, private collection), the colour combination is ungainly, the white on top of the yellow is particularly odd. In *Untitled* (1957, Zurich), as in *Number 16* (1958), white is used to separate two closely valued colours: in the former case, two coppery oranges which're delicately inflected with yellow. It is as a harmonizer between two closely valued colours that the white band works best in Rothko's 1950s canvases, as in *White Band (Number 27*, 1954, Ben Heller, New York). In *Untitled* (1955, collection: Grahamn Gund) white hogs the whole of the larger lower form; the upper one, in orange, is separated by the white mass by a narrow band of red. Yet the predominance of white does not appear gawky, as in *White, Red on Yellow*.

When Mark Rothko scumbles the white shapes at the edges, the transition from white to the surrounding colours is more gradual and thus enables the severity of white to be toned down. It is not in Rothko's style to produce many predominantly white paintings, as with, say, Robert Ryman, or Morris Louis (Louis's acres of 'white' is of course the bare cotton duck canvas).

In *Light, Earth and Blue* (1954, private collection), for example, the upper shape is creamy white and expands to take over two thirds of the painting. Yet the edges are thoroughly dabbed over with the background colour (light grey-cyan), so the rectangle is not rigid and unequivocal. The expanse of azure in the underlying rectangle, too, alters and softens the dominion of the white. Is the white rectangle a doorway or gateway to some transcendent zone? Is it a blank, blocked window, as out of Michelangelo Buonaroti's Laurentian Library? Is it a cloud riding in the sky, or reflected on the ocean?

1962's *Blue and Grey*, which consists of, as expected, mostly blue and grey, is another irregular rectangle of white over a smaller rectangle of dark blue. Here, though, the white is really a mixture of grey and cream, which, as in *Number 18* (1951, private collection, Utica, New York, at least the third painting with this title), there is an enormous rectangle of white dominating the painting. It is easy to see this white form as having a representational equivalent in the natural world. It recalls nothing less than a glowing portion of the sky. This simultaneously banal and transcendent interpretation is enhanced by the 'horizon' of this white sky, which is a relatively solid line, below the halfway mark. The top of the white rectangle is thinned out into the red background.

If one wanted to be apocalyptic, one might see this white sky in *Number 18* as an abstract vision of the distant glow of a sunrise, or a World War Two bombardment at night, or the light of a thousand suns of the atomic bomb on Hiroshima. Mentioning Hiroshima in connection with Mark Rothko is a kind of banality in itself, a too easy appropriation of a cataclysmic and horrific historical event in the cause of a tired art critic's response to a New York artist's painting. It's lazy to merge Rothko's art with Hiroshima or the concentration camps. It self-aggrandizes the critic and the artist.

RED AND BLACK

Towards the end of the 1950s, when Mark Rothko started working on his mural commissions, there are a number of paintings which mix red and black, but not as severely or as closely as the murals. Canvases such as *Light Red Over Black* (1957, Tate Modern), *Brown and Black in Reds* (1958, private collection), *Grayed Olive Green, on Maroon* (1961, Washington), *Orange, Red and Red* (1962, Dallas Museum of Art, Texas), and *Untitled* (1963, Estate of Mark Rothko) are distinctly darker than paintings of the early 1950s. Even as he mixed in more and more black into his colour patterns, Rothko kept his colours vibrant. *Light Red Over Black*, for example, depicts two large rectangular forms of black, but the scarlet that is brushed in around the black shapes is so radiant, it cancels any melancholy or 'negative' connotations the blacks might generate. *Brown and Black in Reds* consists of two dark forms, the upper narrow rectangle in mid-brown, and the large rectangle in near-black, but these are overwhelmed by a swamp of red, scarlet at the centre, a deeper alizarin crimson towards the base of the painting.

Even the dimmest of Mark Rothko's 1950s paintings, such as *Grayed Olive Green, on Maroon*, are set alive by Rothko's careful arrangements of a variety of reds. *Black, Ochre, Red Over Red* (1957, collection: Panza di Biumo, Milan) is structured around the dramatic form of three of Rothko's 'things' which are weighted down by the solid black form at the top. The dark tone so high up in the vertical format painting gives the work an unusual sense of being top-heavy. The reds underneath it, however, are larger and quite adequate to support the black rectangle.

A comparable work, of a year before, *White Cloud* (1956, private collection), which is the reverse of *Black, Ochre, Red Over Red* (a smaller white rectangle over a huge red ground), shows how powerful the colour red can be, how it can carry any other colours with it, if there is enough of it.

Within the colour red, Mark Rothko showed that he could use slightly lighter and slightly darker tones of the same red and make a painting work. *Four Reds* (1957, collection: Daniel Schwarz) is one of those paintings which demonstrates Rothko's mastery of lightening and darkening a single colour.

When the whole painting seems to be composed of very dark areas of colour, as in *Number 9* (1958, collection: Donald Blinken), a narrow ribbon of vermilion at the very top of the painting serves to ignite the work and kick away 'negative' or melancholy connotations. There are some other paintings which use this technique, notably *Painting* (1961, Museum of Fine Arts, Houston), in which a thinned-out carnation red modulates masses of cobalt on indigo.

One of my favourite Mark Rothko paintings, which has the highly poetic name of *Number 118* (1961, collection: Kunst-sammlung Nordrhein-Westfalen, Düsseldorf) features a narrow band of brilliant carmine above immense fields of very dark ultramarine. This is a large work (115 x 102.5 inches) and one of Rothko's most powerful. But the feelings generated by *Number 118* are not at all of being overwhelmed or saddened. There are passages in this painting, as in most of Rothko's paintings, that thrill the viewer. For example, that little patch of azure in the midst of the smouldering ultramarine of the lower rectangle. Or the way the ribbon of rose red bleeds away at its ends into the mid-mauve background. As a sensual evocation of colour, *Number 118* is superb: it is one of those canvases that negates the habitual reading of Rothko as a dark, 'tragic' artist. Though it is one of Rothko's darkest pictures, visually, outside of the Seagram or Houston murals, it has an inner radiance that is undeniably attractive.

VI

SACRED SPACES:
THE ROTHKO CHAPELS
AND MURALS

It was practically inevitable that Mark Rothko should produce paintings to decorate a chapel (other artists who have had church, chapel and cathedral commissions include Jean Cocteau, Marc Chagall, Brice Marden and Henri Matisse). Indeed, Rothko's paintings have become the focal point of the Rothko Chapel in Houston, Texas. This Chapel, and other Rothko 'chapels', such as the 'Rothko Room' at the Tate Modern in London, are seen as Mark Rothko's greatest achievements.[1] The effects that Rothko's paintings seem to aim for – quietness, authority, humility, tragedy, spirituality – are also the qualities treasured in religion, and in particular in Judæo-Christianity. These are the emotional qualities one associates with being in a church or monastery: spacious interiors, lit with a soft, diffuse light, smooth stone floors, whitewashed walls, a dim sense of the outside world, and a feeling of sanctity. These are the spaces – in the cathedral, the chapel, the monk's cell – that are intended to induce contemplation, interiority, self-enclosure, holiness.

In taking on the commissions, Mark Rothko approached them in the thoughtful, considerate manner of the Renaissance painter. He knew well and loved the Early Renaissance artists, in particular Fra Angelico. It is no accident that Rothko's Chapel and the mural series recall the chapels and monasteries decorated by painters such as Giotto, Masaccio and Angelico. With the Houston commission, Rothko stated his intention was to 'make East and West merge in an octagonal chapel' (D. Ashton, 1983, 169).

One of the key reference points for the Rothko chapels is Fra Angelico's beautiful series of frescoes at San Marco in Florence. Mark Rothko was aware of creating a series of paintings which would have a common theme, as with Angelico's frescoes. Created in a very secular world, where the sense of the profound is lost amidst the conspicuous consumption of late capitalism, Rothko's Houston paintings are a version of the Passion.

Mark Rothko was not new to creating specifically Christian images. He had painted pictures of the Crucifixion and Gethsemane in the 1930s and 1940s. It is wholly in keeping with Rothko's personality, as it is perceived in art criticism, to create a series of paintings which were abstract equivalents for the Passion of Christ. Not a few critics have seen correspondences with Barnett Newman's *Stations of the Cross* series of paintings: both were New York School abstract meditations on emotions and themes some of which corresponded or alluded to the Christian Passion. Although Newman and Rothko are different artists, Newman is probably the artist closest to Rothko in many ways. A study of Rothko's Houston and Seagram mural series and Barnett Newman's *Stations of the Cross* would require another book. Critics have dealt with the correspondences and differences elsewhere.[2]

Barnett Newman's *Stations of the Cross* paintings are different in some key formal respects from Mark Rothko's Houston Chapel and mural series: the reference to the Christian Stations, for example, was only one of many allusions Newman wanted to make (he also used the Old Testament, Greek mythology, the *Qabbalah* and Jewish religion). Each of Newman's *Stations* uses the same format (6.5 by 5 foot canvases, with the bands and 'zips' in the same place, painted mainly in black, with some white paint), while Rothko's are determinedly sombre and dark, without any lighter tones, and in a variety of sizes and proportions. Even within his tight set of formal components, Newman works out many variants: in *The First Station*, a black stripe on the left is disturbed by a roughly daubed stripe on the right. The loose brushmarks of the right-hand 'zip' upset the steady equilibrium of the area of black and white paint on the left-hand side of the painting. In subsequent *Stations* this right-hand 'zip' settles down somewhat, to become a very narrow black stripe in *The Fifth Station*. At this point, though, the left-hand black stripe, which has been in a state of passivity up 'til now, suddenly deliquesces, its edge becoming fractured.

By *The Twelfth* and *Thirteenth Station*, the black has enveloped most of the canvas, so that, in the penultimate *Station*, the configuration of white and black of the first *Stations* has been reversed. Although Barnett Newman employed the potent phrase *lema sabachthani*, the allusions to the Christian Passion are much stronger in Mark Rothko's mural series and 'chapels' than in Newman's *Stations of the Cross*. Both Rothko's and Newman's series of paintings, though, were about the importance of (religious) faith, of the subjectivity and intensity of being a pilgrim, someone on a quest for something transcendent, something Beyond, timeless, unknown, eternal. The cry *lema sabachthani* was the 'question that has no answer', said Newman, a cry of despair (and also exaltation) that is uttered outwards, into the darkness (of ignorance, alienation, Godlessness) that surrounds the modern soul.

Barnett Newman's emphasis on religious awe in art manifested itself in his sculptures. He traded on the mystifying, gravity-defying aspect of sculpture in his *Broken Obelisk*, which is a pillar balancing on the tip of a pyramid. The balancing of the steel column is a technical *tour-de-force*, a piece of bravado that is gendered because Newman conceived of the two forms as masculine and feminine. Guess which one is on top: the male. In a similar way, Constantin Brancusi conceived his *Adam and Eve* sculpture as one form on top of the other. Guess which one was on top. In Newman's and Brancusi's sculpture, the male element is nearer the sky, it is spiritual, transcendent, ascendant, superior. The feminine element is underneath, closer to the earth, a squat, nurturing figure which holds up the male's balancing act.

Broken Obelisk trades religious imagery from the ancient world (Egypt, in the Pyramids, and Jericho) and from mediæval Europe (Chartres). What Barnett Newman said of *Broken Obelisk* – 'it is concerned with life and I hope I have transformed its tragic content into a glimpse of the sublime'[3] – could have been uttered by Mark Rothko (in reference to his murals, for instance). Like so many of Newman's paintings, his *Broken Obelisk* is conceived as an act of faith, a flame in the darkness. Like Constantin Brancusi's *Birds in Space*, Newman's sculpture aims to soar heavenward in some ultimate act of earthly transcendence.[4]

Mark Rothko's Houston Chapel murals are the tightest and most carefully controlled of the murals series. The colours are extremely close. Rothko meticulously restricted the amount of light the murals emitted, and the amount of light they would absorb. It is easy to understand how viewers speak of the 'subliminal' or 'transcendent' qualities of the Houston Chapel murals. There seems to be hardly anything in them, to grasp onto. At least in Claude Monet's *Waterlilies* the viewer can always return to nature, to the shapes of the lilies and the reflections on the water. In Monet's art, one can find the way back to nature and the world. Rothko's Houston Chapel paintings invite a different sort of participation. His murals invite the viewer to lose themselves in the paintings, thereby losing themselves to themselves, in themselves. That is, the paintings are not the final stage in the participants' (religious) project. They can't be. Art in churches, religious art in general, is not the endpoint. One must not get stuck on the art object, but on what the art object is trying to evoke, or point towards. In the case of Rothko's murals, which is church art like Renaissance altarpieces were church art, the viewer is invited to go beyond the paintings and ponder on holiness within and without the self.

To make sure viewers, positioned by the church context as pilgrims or initiates, would not get stuck on the paintings themselves, Mark Rothko made them his most abstract and reduced images. There are no easy to identify architectural forms, as in the Harvard murals, or even vaguely discernible gateways, as in the Seagram murals. Instead, the Houston murals consist of coloured panels, of dark red and red-black. Emptied of recognizable imagery, the Houston murals become an ambience or context in which the visitor can meditate, pray, dream, whatever. It is the *context* of the chapel that is important, just as much if not more than the 'content' of the paintings themselves. Religious art works very much in terms of context, on the building and its significance. Wandering into S. Agostino church in the back streets of Rome, for example, one can just about perceive the dark forms of a Caravaggio painting in the dim candleshine. The context of being in the shadowy, incense-rich interior of the church does much of the work in encouraging a religious response to the artwork.

Similarly with Mark Rothko's Houston Chapel, which provides an atmosphere for prayer, which became Rothko's goal.[5] Rothko's Houston murals evoke certain proportions and rhythms, an atmosphere of ambiguous colour, which eschews theological dogma. Rothko is not making a particular ecumenical/ theological point with these murals. Instead, he evokes, in non-representational but powerful ways, a religious atmosphere, which one can associate with Byzantine icons, incense-filled Greek Orthodox churches, the Catholic fervour of churches in Brazil or Spain, or the synagogues of Rothko's motherland, Russia. Or going back further, in certain cloudy illumination on dull days, the Rothko Rooms may evoke the palæolithic caves and underground vaults which pre-date Christianity, or Hebraic religion, or ancient Greece.

The intangible, abstract spaces of Mark Rothko's Houston murals have an aura about them (in them) of primal religion, the animism which predates organized or monotheic religion. This interpretation is possible because Rothko leaves the paintings open: one can read anything one likes into them. They are mirrors, just like the face of God is a mirror.

Mark Rothko claimed he was only interested in proportion and shape in the Houston murals. He spoke of the duality of the murals, which would evoke both the finite and infinite. Ad Reinhardt is another Abstract Expressionist whose five-foot square black canvases with their dim cruciform shapes recall the Houston murals. Reinhardt's project was equally 'religious' like Rothko's – Reinhardt wrote at length of Zen, Taoism, Buddhism, the dark night of the soul of Christianity, the dark-on-dark of Meister Eckhart, *The Cloud of Unknowing*, St John of the Cross, Mother Night, and so on.

Ad Reinhardt's square black paintings can be seen as equivalents for this kind of religious darkness, which was defined by Reinhardt in countless notes and essays with the terms of Buddhism 'not this, not that'. 'I'm just making the last paintings anyone can make', said Ad Reinhardt.[6] This extract from Reinhardt's unpublished notes is typical, and defines not only his own form of painting, but also that of other 'Northern' painters such as Mark Rothko, Barnett Newman, Christopher Le Brun, Thérèse Oulton, Brice Marden and Anselm Keifer:

"Northern" preferences for black medium
"Black," medium of the mind
Puritan, self-righteous, self-criticism
Conscience of a bad conscience
Luminous darkness, true light, evanescence
"Him that has made the dark his hiding place"
"Flight of the lone to the alone"
Perfection, central, cohesive, purifying principle
Polemic, dogmatic, scriptural (1991, 90)

Ad Reinhardt's writings are sometimes pretentious and

portentous, quite different from Barnett Newman's matter-of-fact statements, or Joseph Cornell's wistful, dreamy diaries. Reinhardt, for example, discarded the 'religious' monicker, and disliked the allusions viewers made to Islam, Christianity, Buddhism and Hinduism when discussing his paintings (even though he wrote about religion more than almost any other contemporary painter). Reinhardt even stated that 'painting really has no relation to any of the religions nor ever has' (1991, 14). This is an extraordinary outburst from a well-read artist, for art since earliest times has been associated deeply with religion, and much of the greatest art made in the latest 100,000 years has been in the service of religion.

Ad Reinhardt's black paintings were all called *Abstract Painting, Black*. He dubbed them '[c]lassical black-square uniform five-foot timeless trisected evanescences of the sixties'.[7] They were meant to be formless (but they weren't), lightless (they couldn't be), spaceless (not possible), changeless (they were not), and relationless (they were full of relations, internally, and were related to countless other works of art). Reinhardt's paintings were sensual where he wanted them to be beyond sensuality; they were never completely imageless because Reinhardt insisted on the cruciform shape. Richard Stankiewicz wrote of them: '[t]he extraordinary object, the one with presence, is one which is subjectively and tyrannically there… It is the ultimate realism, this presence'.[8]

For all his exaltation of Oriental mystical precepts, his insistence on the radical reductionism of his art, his belief in black as negation, 'pure non-being', his desire to 'push painting beyond its thinkable, seeable, feelable limits', Ad Reinhardt's abstract black paintings were not the last paintings to be made, or that could be made. In his quest for an imageless, relationless, timeless art, Reinhardt was doomed to failure, for despite his insistence on the immateriality of his quest, the painter is always deeply entrenched in the materiality of painting. The difficulty was evoking the void using physical objects. As Barnett Newman said:

'[e]mptiness is not that easy. The point is to produce it with paint.'[9]

Ad Reinhardt's task of describing the indescribable with the halfway decent means of paint was bound to fail. The quest for delimitation and non-representation was much stronger in the art of Reinhardt than in Mark Rothko: Reinhardt kept up with the *Abstract Paintings, Black* for some seven years, from the end of the 1950s to his death in 1967. For Harold Rosenberg, Reinhardt was 'a drier logician than Rothko', and Rothko would not follow Reinhardt's reductionism to its radical finality (1972). Rothko commented on Ad Reinhardt thus:

> The difference between me and Reinhardt is that he's a mystic. By that I mean that his paintings are immaterial. Mine are *here*. Materially. The surfaces, the work of the brush and so on. His are untouchable[10]

The ironic thing is that Ad Reinhardt's paintings were no more immaterial or 'untouchable' than those of Mark Rothko. Furthermore, what people think of Reinhardt also applies very much to Rothko: there are many points of contact between the two painters. What is said by critics of Reinhardt's art can apply to Rothko's, and vice versa. Reinhardt's black square paintings as a project can be helpfully compared with Rothko's murals series. Reinhardt's lifelong friend, the mystic Thomas Merton, wrote of the disappearance of the self in God, which could apply equally to Reinhardt's and Rothko's paintings (think of the Houston murals): '[s]o it is with one who has vanished into God by pure contemplation. God alone is left'.[11]

The theologian Paul Tillich said of Reinhardt's work that it depicts the 'non-representational expression of mystic depths of experience.'[12] Again, these thoughts could easily apply to Mark Rothko. Reinhardt's black paintings and Rothko's Houston murals do mark the end of a certain strain of painting, which might be said to go back to Matthias Grünewald and Early Netherlandish painters such as Rogier van der Weyden. It is a thread of Northern European painting which descends into the shadows

(Rembrandt van Rijn, Georges de La Tour and Frans Hals), of which Rothko and Reinhardt can be seen as the last flowering. Other painters did not agree that 'painting was dead', that there was nothing else to do. Jasper Johns remarked that painters continue to work, while Helen Frankenthaler said in 1970: 'I think there's still a lot more to do in abstract painting' (E. De Antonio, 161).

The accounts of Mark Rothko's creation of the mural series record how much time he spent just sitting in front of his paintings and musing. Often he would sit and contemplate the stretchers, even before the canvas had been stretched on them. Observers of Leonardo da Vinci at work in Milan described how the Italian Renaissance master would sit and stare at his *Last Supper* for hours on end, sometimes leaving it for a few days, then returning to dab at it for a moment, then leaving again. Matteo Bandello recalled:

> It was his habit, as I myself have witnessed and observed on several occasions, to come here in the early hours of the morning and mount the scaffolding, for the *Cenacolo* is somewhat high above the ground; he was accustomed (I say) to remain there brush in hand from sunrise to sunset, forgetting to eat or drink, painting continually. Then he might stay away for two, three or four days without setting hand to it, or he would remain in front of it for one or two hours and contemplate it in solitude, examining and criticizing to himself the figures he had created. I have also seen him (as caprice or fancy took hold of him) departing in the middle of the day when the sun was in Leo from the Corte Vecchia, where he was working on his stupendous clay Horse and he would come straight to Delle Grazie; and he would climb the scaffolding, seize a brush, apply a brush stroke or two to one of the figures, and suddenly depart and go elsewhere. (In R. Payne, 1979, 14)

In the traditional manner, Mark Rothko used rabbit skin glue to size the canvas, mixing in dry pigment, with oil and turpentine. The grounds were mixed with alizarin crimson and black. Then Rothko began to arrange the doorway shapes. At times, he would alter the composition by a quarter of an inch: this shows how crucial the placement of the forms were, for a quarter of an inch on a fifteen foot canvas is a tiny proportion. The proportions had to be exactly right: the murals are a complex interrelation of sizes, edges and interior forms. According to Robert Motherwell, Rothko was very secretive about his working methods. Apparently, he used to work from dawn (5 am) until 10 am. Rothko put a parachute over the skylight of his studio – an effect which was reproduced in subsequent Rothko 'chapels', such as at the Tate Modern in London (but he also admitted to using high intensity lights which were arranged like stage lights in a theatre).[13]

The Harvard murals are easily the most 'expressive', gesturally, of the three mural series (the Harvard, Seagram/ Tate and Houston Chapel murals). The Harvard murals (1962) are large, as in the grand Abstract Expressionist tradition (104.8 inches inches high by widths such as 96, 180.5 and 117 inches). The post-and-lintel forms are much clearer than in the Seagram paintings: these paintings more directly recall, in their inner architectural forms, the blank windows of the Michelangelo-Medici Library in Florence. The colour and tonal values of the Harvard murals are the widest of the three mural series. They are the loosest and most 'open' of the murals.

Some critics have seen the murals as the apotheosis of Mark Rothko's art; for others, they are a failure. When Rothko dropped his luminous colour and concentrated on the two colours, black and red, some critics felt he had jettisoned what made his art so effective. Instead of an intensification, there is a lessening of power. There are no colours against which the black-reds can work, and harmonize. The lack of secondary colours means the main colours have to do all the work themselves. Without the dark blue or purple or orange backgrounds, the 'things' of the murals have nowhere else to go but to refer to themselves. The negation/ deletion/ reduction of colour is also a limitation of the artist's tools of expression. In limiting his colours the artist may be plunging himself into a self-negation. For some critics, the dark reds 'do not permit very much resonance at all' (M. Kozloff, 1961). The technical reductionism may force Rothko into a corner out of which he cannot manœuvre himself. Instead of extending colour, there may be a chromatic dead-end: painting as a kind of invisibility. What this results in is the paintings become opaque, do not allow the viewer to enter them and move around. Instead of a welcoming glow they offer a wall of solid, impenetrable oil paint. Emptiness becomes a wall. This is where Rothko's murals become forbidding and tragic, because they oppress or prevent transcendence. This relates to Rothko's impression of the Michelangelo Laurentian Library in Florence. Michelangelo, Rothko said

> makes the viewers feel that they are trapped in a room where all the doors and windows are bricked up, so that all they can do is butt their heads forever against the wall. (in J. Fischer, 16)

Here Mark Rothko's scenario becomes a horror story scene, with the viewers of his murals feeling bricked up with no way out. Of course, Rothko's reading of Michelangelo's architecture says much about his state of mind, but it also adds a flavour of the macabre to his project with his murals. One can interpret Rothko's many commands for the exhibition of his pictures, his demands for lighting and having his large paintings shown in small rooms as an authoritarian attempt to produce a claustrophobic environment, in which the viewer is not allowed any let-up from being immersed in the paintings. It is as if Rothko wants the viewer to experience something of the same suffering that he himself underwent in making the pictures. It's as if he's saying, 'I've suffered – now it's your turn!' And galleries follow this project with sanctimonious diligence, taking care not to hang Rothko's works too near other artists' works. At times, Rothko's paintings are approached with the servile unctuousness of over-zealous acolytes.

The Tate Gallery paintings were originally made for the Four Seasons restaurant in the Seagram Building on Park Avenue in

New York City.[14] The building, designed by architect Philip Johnson, was a big, prestigious structure, and the commission was an important one for Mark Rothko. There were many stories as to exactly why Rothko decided not to allow his paintings to be displayed in the restaurant. One story had Rothko originally understanding that the restaurant would be used by the people who worked in the building, a staff canteen or boardroom, and refusing to fulfil the commission when he found out otherwise. Philip Johnson asserted that Rothko always knew it was going to be a public restaurant. Another story (related by his daughter Kate and friend Dan Rice) had Rothko visiting the restaurant for a meal with his wife, and being outraged by the place (and the food). Whatever the truth, the Four Seasons restaurant was destined not to be the first 'Rothko Room'.

The Tate Gallery's 'Rothko Room' came about when the director of the Tate, Norman Reid, visited Mark Rothko in the city that never sleeps in the mid-1960s. After some further visits, it was decided that Rothko would consider giving some of his paintings to the museum (donations which could be set off against the tax). In the event, Rothko chose nine paintings from some thirty which had been painted for the Seagram commission. Rothko selected them specifically so they would work as a group. A scale model of the room the Tate Gallery had earmarked for the Rothko paintings was delivered to Rothko: he worked out how to display the paintings (using small sketches). One of his unusual decisions was to mount one of the large paintings above another. As with his other installations, Rothko had very precise instructions as to lighting, fittings, mounting, decoration, wall colour and so on.

The Seagram paintings are full of suggestions of architectural shapes – in particular, posts and lintels, doorways. The affinities between the Seagram paintings and Greek temples and Roman architecture (such as the House of Mysteries in Pompeii) is apparent. Another affinity is to Michelangelo's Laurentian Library in Florence, a space which lingered in Mark Rothko's memory as he worked on the Seagram murals.[15]

Noting the Medici Library in Florence, the Fra Angelico frescoes at San Marco, the Greek temple at Paestum, the House of Mysteries at Pompeii, does nothing, however, to help 'explain' or perceive the Seagram/ Tate Gallery murals. No amount of meditation on Angelico's beautiful Thomist paintings at San Marco gets the viewer any closer to the Seagram paintings. The viewer can consider the kind of cultural references Mark Rothko may have been conscious of during the paintings' manufacture; one can ponder on Rothko's mood, but this does not make the paintings any clearer. They retain their mystery, because they are exceptionally dense works.

Trying to describe exactly what one sees in the Tate Modern Rothkos is not that easy, either, but it is what the spectator sees that really counts, that Mark Rothko was really concerned with. The murals are entitled *Black on Maroon* or *Red on Maroon* but that doesn't help any. What strikes one immediately about the Seagram murals is their very large scale: each *Black/ Red on Maroon* is some 90-105 inches high: some are 81 inches wide, others are a massive 180 inches (15 feet) wide.

Shown together as a group, the Seagram paintings make their presence known in an unequivocal manner. In these paintings, Mark Rothko explored very closely valued colour; the colours hover between the two existential colours of life, black (death, the unknown, invisible, divine) and red (passion, blood, heart, anger). The combination of the colours, which always return to a dark red or maroon, and the large scale of the canvases, suggest an atmosphere of solemnity, passion, death, mourning, trans-cendence. Here comes the slew of adjectives!

But what is striking *is* the serious tone of the Seagram murals, the heavy, velvety darkness of them, like the drapes or hangings in a church, or the colour of the sky in the background of Renaissance *Crucifixions*, when, at the ninth hour, Jesus gives up the ghost, and the clouds turn a swollen, bruised black and purple. The colour of the Seagram murals might also be suitable for the scene of Christ's interrogation by Pontius Pilate. One can imagine the scene on stage or in a movie where Pilate and the messiah meet being lit with this maroon and black colour. It is easy to see how these paintings can be equivalents for the night of the Crucifixion. The effect is also like the interior of a church or a synagogue, the air heavy with incense. The churchy atmosphere is wholly appropriate, with its suggestions of candlelight, rituals of Mass and sacrifice, blood and fire, a shadowy gloom. Rothko was conscious of 'making a place' with his paintings: that is, he intended his paintings to create a whole environment: large paintings in a small space.

Looking now at the forms and shapes Mark Rothko depicted in his Seagram murals, one sees gateways or doorways. A broad open rectangle in a slightly lighter red is floated upon a darker red in the vertical format and one of the horizontal *Red on Maroon* paintings. In the two huge, landscape format *Red on Maroons* (both 1959), a darker crimson or maroon is placed upon a lighter red or maroon. These little words – *red, maroon, doorway* – do not describe, however, the immense scale of the paintings. The forms are not rigid, linear rectangles: they are curved or diffuse, the broad swathes of paint soften at the edges, as in Rothko's earlier works. Sometimes the gateways have firm outlines, sometimes they bleed into the surround. Sometimes they seem like organic entities, sometimes they are architectural structures. Seen in reproductions, whether in colour or b/w, in posters or prints, Rothko's murals, as with many of his paintings, do not work very well: they need to be confronted physically. This is especially true of the Houston and Seagram murals, where the colour values are so close together. Even the most sophisticated printing techniques cannot reproduce Rothko's subtle mood and colour changes.

The symbolic discourse of the motif of the doorway is inescapable. The doorway is a transitional structure, keeping something out or in, it is a site of transition (or transformation) from one place (or state of being) to another. As soon as one speaks of doorways in paintings and Mark Rothko's art one inevitably ends up at the word 'transcendence'. It is unavoidable, it seems, to start discussing the sense of transcendence from one state to another implied in these paintings.

It is clear from Mark Rothko's statements that he thought of art as a mode of transformation, and that he saw it as a form of transcendence. He spoke of quests, of progression, of moving towards something ('clarity', for example). In the Tate Gallery murals, then, besides the sense of stasis and solemnity, there is a suggestion of movement, from one place to another. The worrying thing is that the doorways in the paintings may actually lead… nowhere. And that Rothko had no idea where he wished the viewer to go. The Laurentian Library of the Medicis in Florence, remember, consisted of 'false' or 'blind' windows: they did not actually look out onto anything. There is no Transcendent Beyond in them, and there might not be in Rothko's Seagram paintings. Instead, as in a monastery (at Fra Angelico's San Marco, for instance), the 'beyond' one is encouraged to move towards is in fact inside oneself.

The function of the San Marco cells is spiritual contemplation. This may also be Mark Rothko's project: to hint at doorways and transcendence, whereas he knows, as mediæval mystics knew, that any form of transcendence begins with the self, with self-transcendence. The point of the Rothko's murals, at Harvard, Houston or London, then, may be to throw the viewer back onto her/ himself. The 'other' or 'beyond' of the Rothko murals must finally reside (as how could it otherwise in the century of Sigmund Freud and psychoanalysis?) in the viewer's own self.

VII

THE LATE GREY, BROWN
AND BLACK WORKS

*I regard as beautiful (historically speaking) all that which, in the most
revered men of an age, assumes visible shape as the expression of what is
most worthy of reverence.*

Friedrich Nietzsche

Many (most) of Mark Rothko's late paintings are entitled *Untitled*.
While in the late 1940s and subsequent works *Untitled* did not
seem so threatening a title, with the late 1960s paintings it
acquires a new foreboding connotation, with Rothko's death
looming at the end of the decade. The last works are a series of
two colour paintings, many of them acrylic on paper. Typically,
the upper colour is black, brown or dark grey; the lower is
usually a mid to light grey. In the late grey/ brown/ black
paintings, the 'dark is always at the top', Rothko said.[1]

The stereotypical interpretation is that these are depressing
works which presage Mark Rothko's death by his own hand.
Surveying the black-and-grey paintings cursorily, one can see
how they can appear melancholy. There is not much to look at, for

a start: the greys and browns are applied in a seemingly uncaring fashion. There is not much that is immediately 'sensuous' about these late paintings, to an eye looking for visual pleasure. If one recalls that in the Houston Chapel murals Rothko said he was concerned not so much with colour but with *proportion* and the relationship between shapes, then these black-and-grey paintings become much clearer. The closer one looks at these late works, the more one sees that Rothko was exploring the same formal aspects that have always concerned painters: the relation between colour and size, scale and shape; the relation between tone and luminosity; the relation between proportion and colour; the relation between surface texture and inner luminescence, and so on.

Take *Untitled* (1969, Estate of Mark Rothko, 2072.69). It is painted in acrylic colour on paper: there are two colours, in a vertical format. The upper colour is a thin brown, swiftly put down onto the paper with a wide brush. The lower mid-grey is more evenly and opaquely applied. The sense of proportion between the two colours is acute: one sees this in all the late black-and-grey works. Sometimes the lower grey rectangle is higher than the mid-way line, sometimes it is lower. In a wide format vertical picture, such as *Brown and Grey* (1969, Estate of Mark Rothko), the grey section is very low down, while in a comparative work, also entitled *Brown and Grey* (1969, private collection), the grey section takes up one third of the painting.

These descriptions of formal characteristics may not satisfy critics who demand that there must be more to painting than that. There is, of course. But the formal aspects of the painting are what concern the painter. For Mark Rothko kept doing these black/ brown/ grey paintings, sometimes with acrylics on paper, sometimes in acrylics on canvas, and sometimes in oil. There was something about them that fascinated him. It had to do partly with the formal considerations such as proportions. The limitation of the palette to black and grey neatly dealt with the problems of colour. The greys and browns were simply painted quickly onto the paper, and the internal organization of each rectangle, the brushstrokes and the thickening or thinning of the paint here and there do not really concern the artist. There is not the same immense care taken over the brushstrokes as on the rectangular canvases of the Fifties, where the way colours merged was crucial. Here, brushstrokes are subordinated to a sense of scale and proportion.

The outer white band, a fraction of an inch wide, was seen by Mark Rothko as important. The border stabilized the inner forms, which are less the 'things' of the multiform paintings, and more like areas of colour. Instead of 'floating' upon radiant coloured grounds or skies, these brown/ black/ grey forms are solidly a part of the painting: they are not going anywhere, they do not have an inner kinetic energy, like the multiforms. The tensions, rather, are between the two main rectangles, and their relationship to the border. The two halves are not a landscape and a sky, though it is tempting to think of them in those terms. What is crucial is the *relationship* between the two coloured areas.

Seen this way, there is nothing sad about the late black-and-grey paper works at all. They can be seen as formal explorations, which is always a large part of painting, from any era, in any place. In a way, the black-and-grey paintings are not as uncompromising as the maroon murals, which offer a much narrower range of tone and colour in which the spectator can move.

The duality or tension between the black and the grey rectangles can be interpreted any which way one chooses: between spirit and matter, spirituality and physicality, mind and body, soul and God, masculine and feminine, past and present, past and future, eternity and now, inner and outer, life and death, and so on. Certainly there is something deeply obsessive about these late works, as with the late works of Vincent van Gogh or J.M.W. Turner, as if there was something Mark Rothko felt he had to get at, somehow, and so he kept working over the form until it offered up its secret knowledge. In this respect, as an alchemical quest, Rothko's late black-brown-grey paper works recall the seven-year project of Ad Reinhardt, compulsively turning out those square black paintings, in the hope of reaching some sublime point, some absolute, some infinity or end zone.

The melancholy interpretation is further debunked by the fact that not all the late works consist of black, brown and grey. There are, for example, light pink paintings, such as *Untitled* (1969, Estate of Mark Rothko, 2069.69). Now this really is a surprise, especially after the previous decade, since the late 1950s, when Mark Rothko's palette (or, more correctly, his bench of tins) darkened. This pink is exceptionally light – it is not the radiant pink of the 1950s works (such as *Number 12*, 1951, private collection). It is a large expanse of shell pink, framed with sky blue behind white. Other paintings include soft grey-pinks below white-greys. Another late acrylic on paper, *Untitled* (1968, Estate of Mary Alice Rothko) is a vertical format work in the old rectangular manner, depicting three white rectangles on a brilliant cardinal ground. The white forms are a return to the 'clouds' of the 1950s. And then, in *Untitled* (1967, private collection), an oil on canvas painting, there is an incredibly bright dark rose-pink form underneath a sonorous mid-red. The painting vies with the Colorfield and Post-Painterly Abstractionists (Jules Olitski, Ellsworth Kelly, Kenneth Noland, Frank Stella, Morris Louis) at their most colourful. one should never forget the elements of wit, humour and irony in Mark Rothko's art: it's not all doom and gloom, it's not all 'tragic', 'religious', 'heroic' and 'transcendent'.

Mark Rothko's art endures for many reasons – it's beautiful (beauty goes a long way), it's emotional, it's intelligent, it's mythical and primal, it's timeless (and hasn't dated at all), and it's multi-purpose: you can read anything you like into those clouds of pure colour.

ILLUSTRATIONS

Works which have influenced Mark Rothko, including the Villa of
Mysteries at Pompeii, Michelangelo's Laurenzian Library, and
Renaissance artists such as Fra Angelico and Mathias Grünewald.

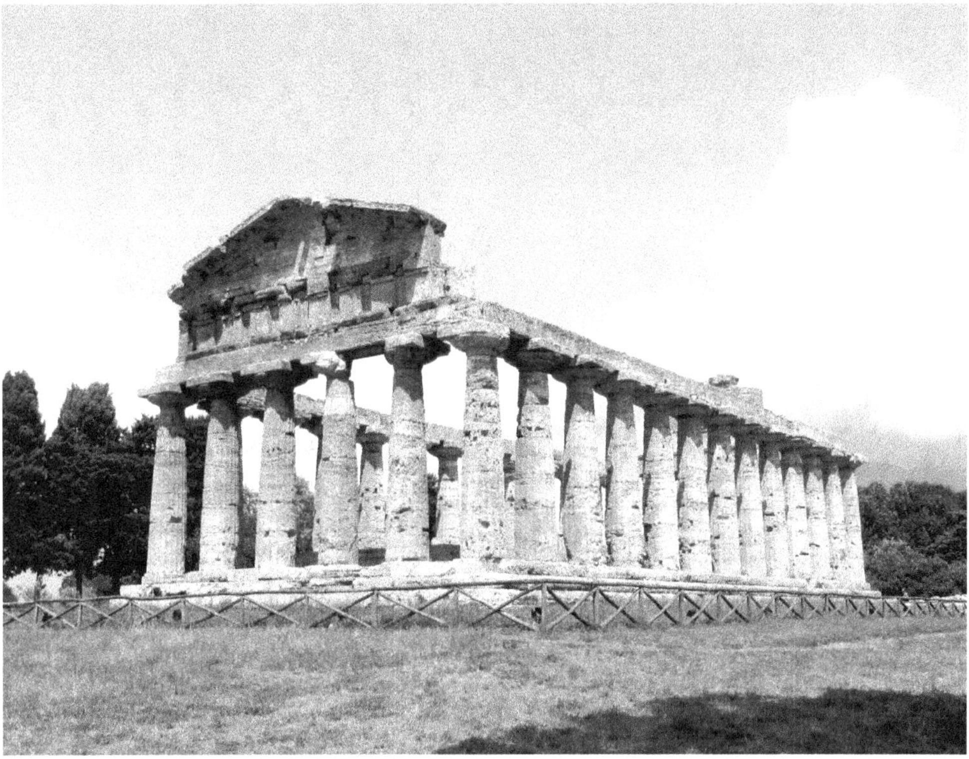

Temples at Paestum

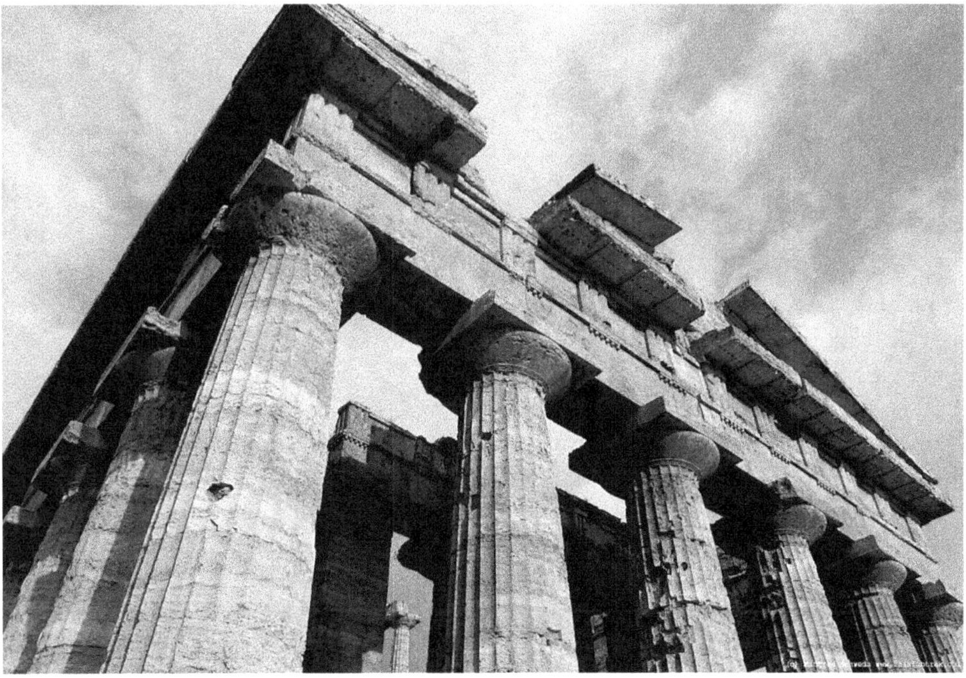

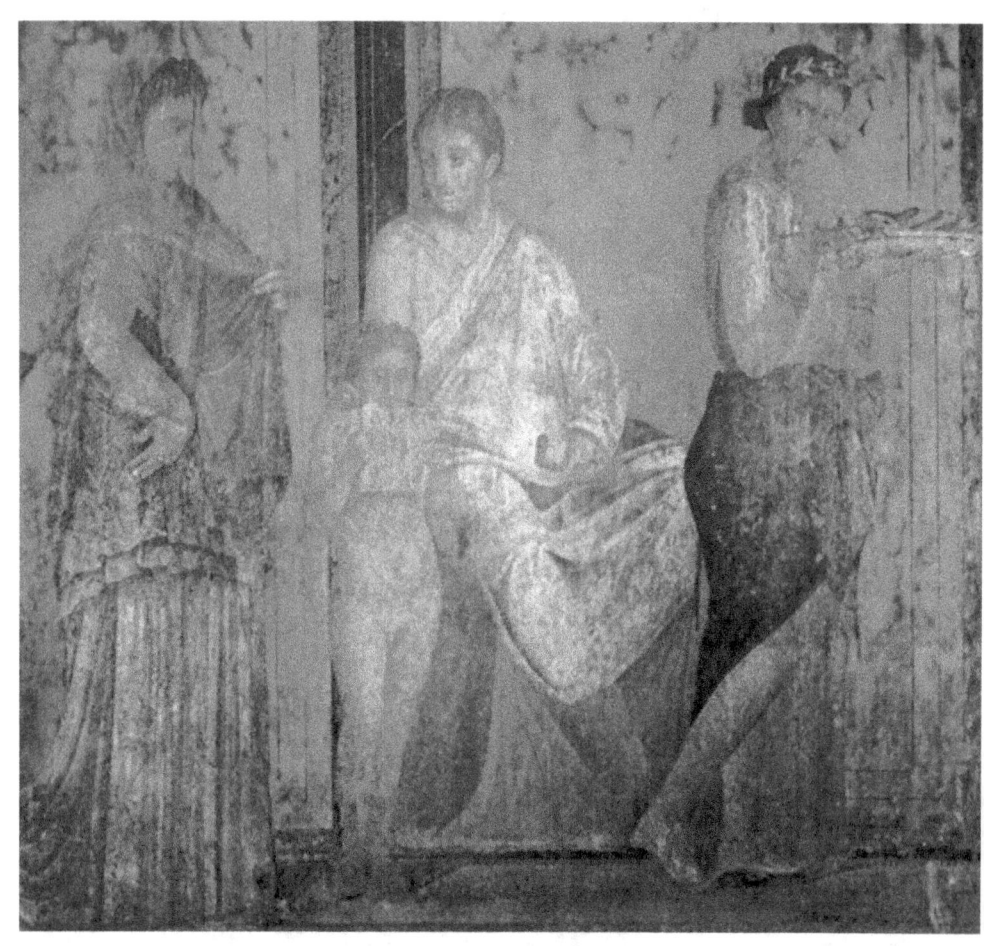

Villa of the Mysteries in Pompeii, c. 50 B.C.

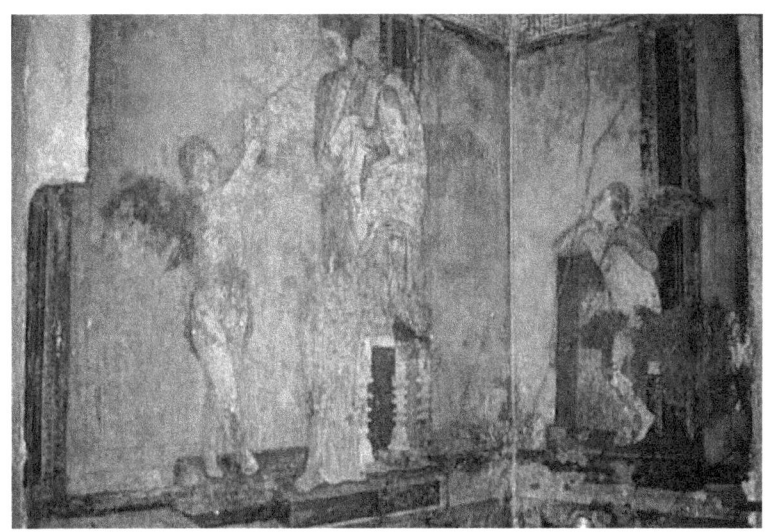

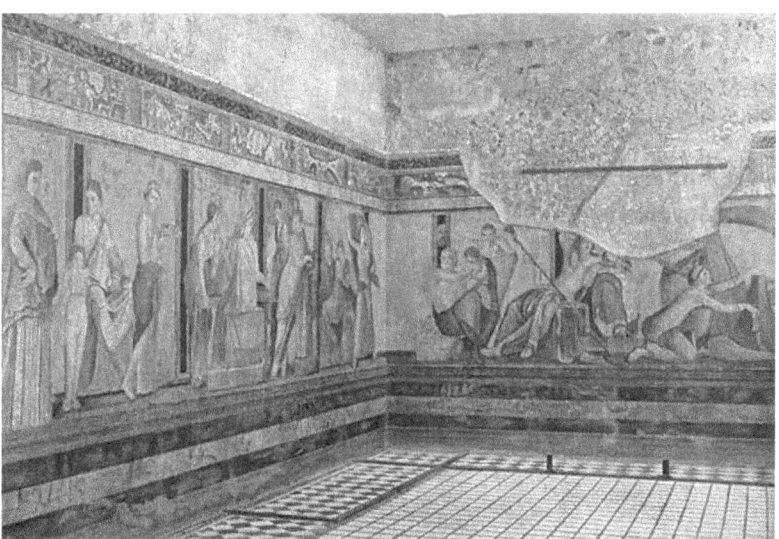

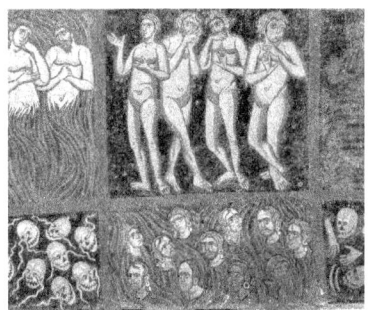

Pompeii, Villa of Mysteries

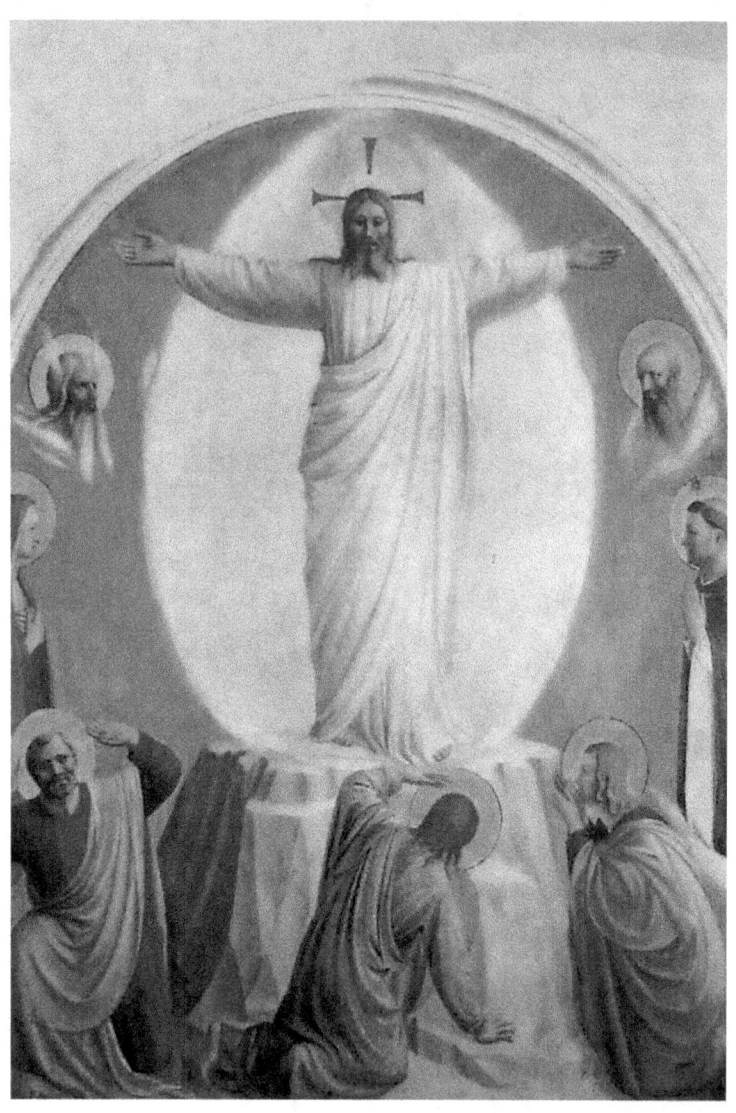

Fra Angelico, The Resurrection, San Marco, Florence

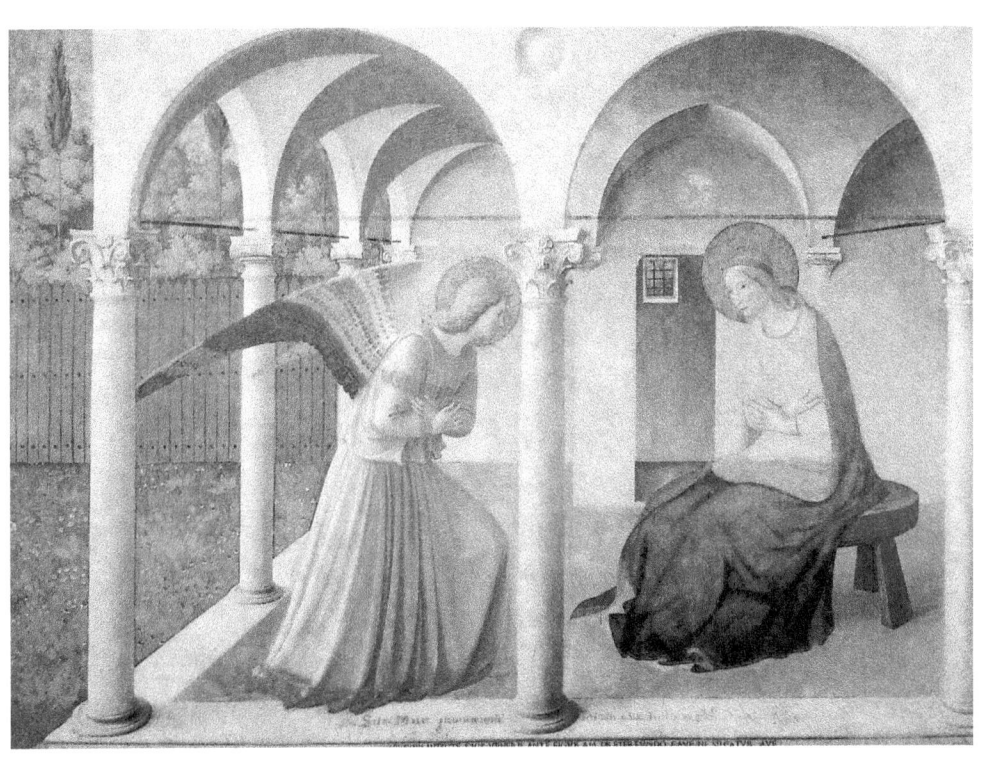

Fra Angelico, The Annunciation, San Marco, Florence

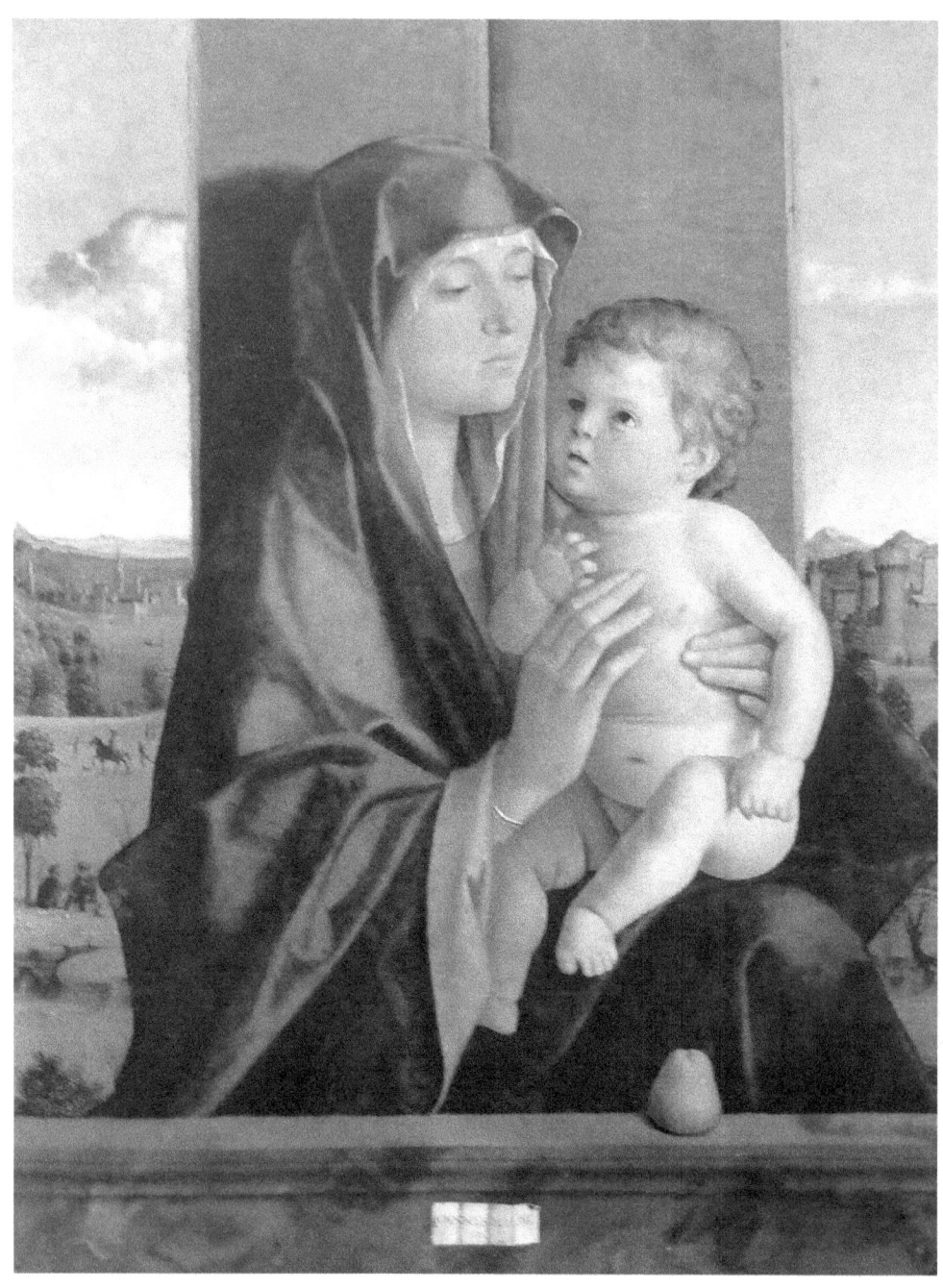

Giovanni Bellini, The Virgin and Child, Bergamo

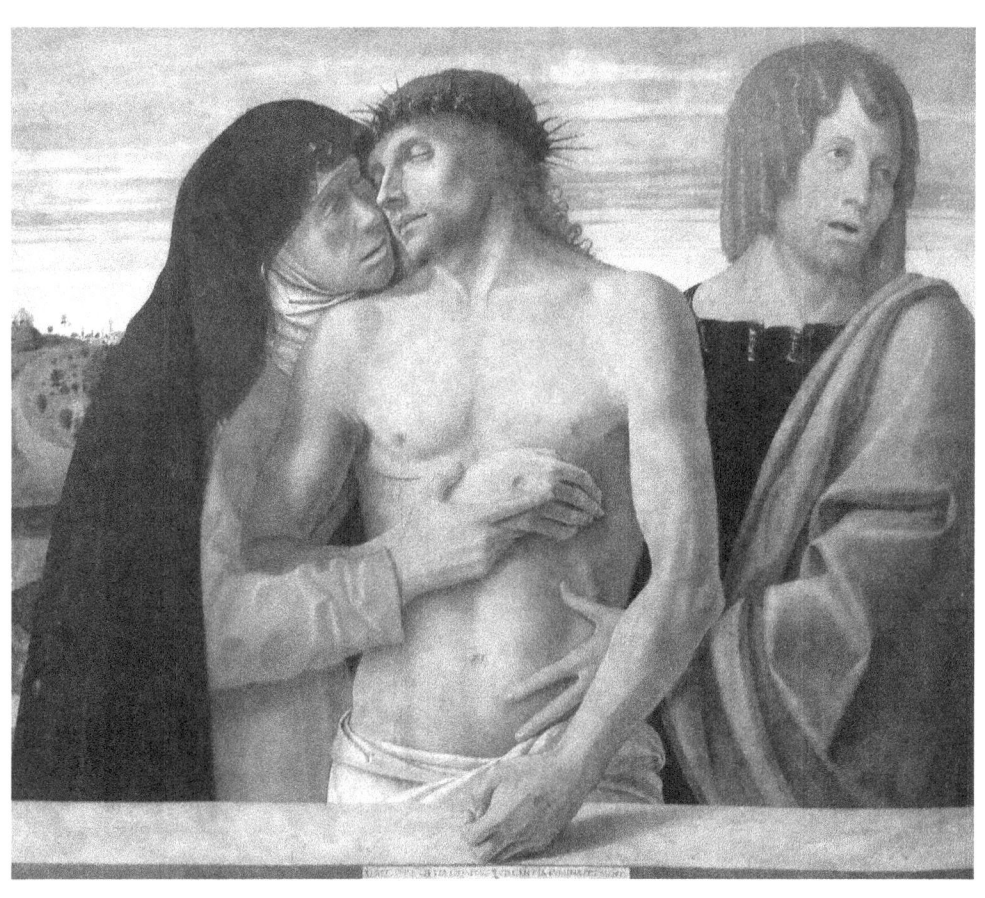

Giovanni Bellini, Pietà, Milan

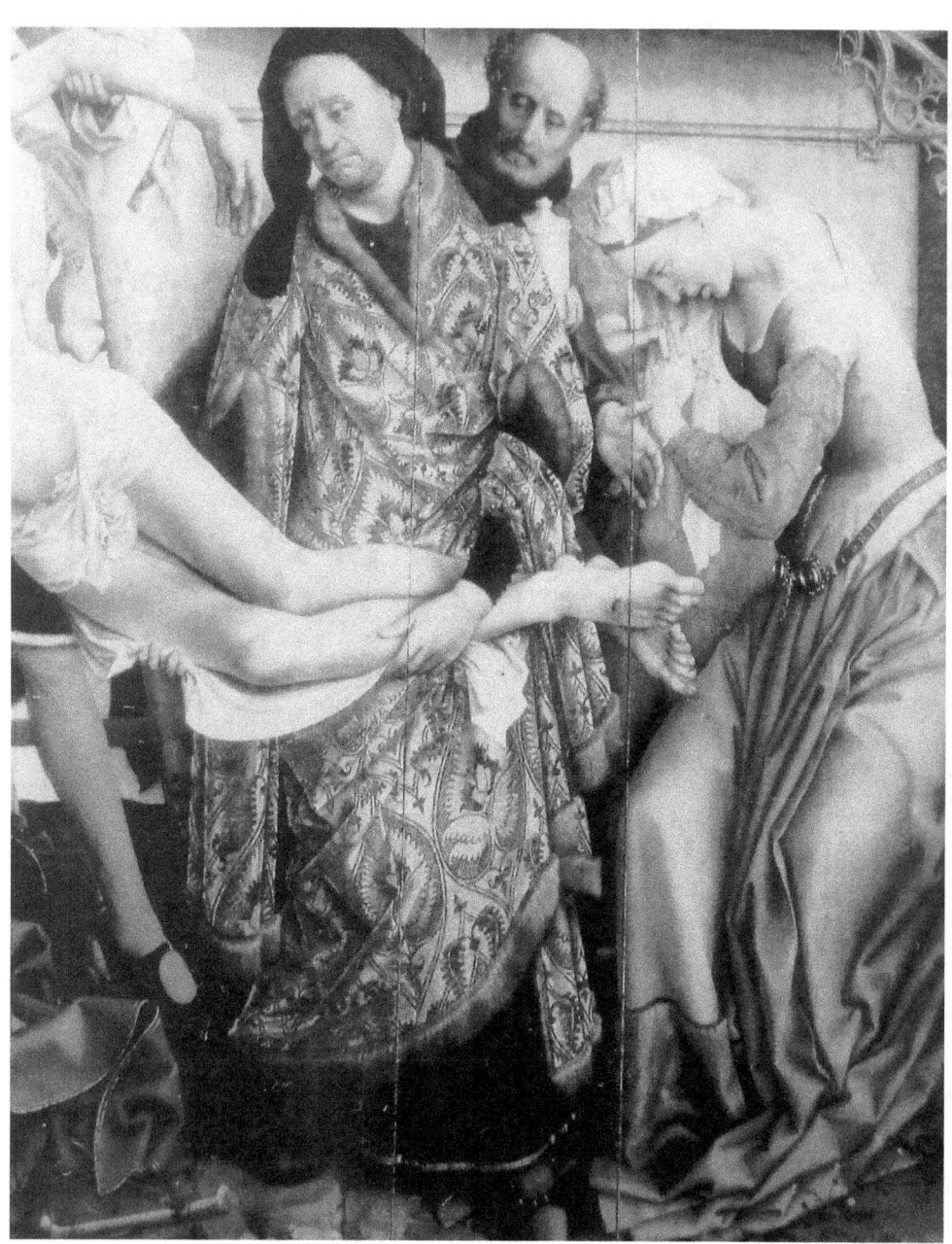

Rogier van der Weyden, Descent From the Cross, detail, Madrid

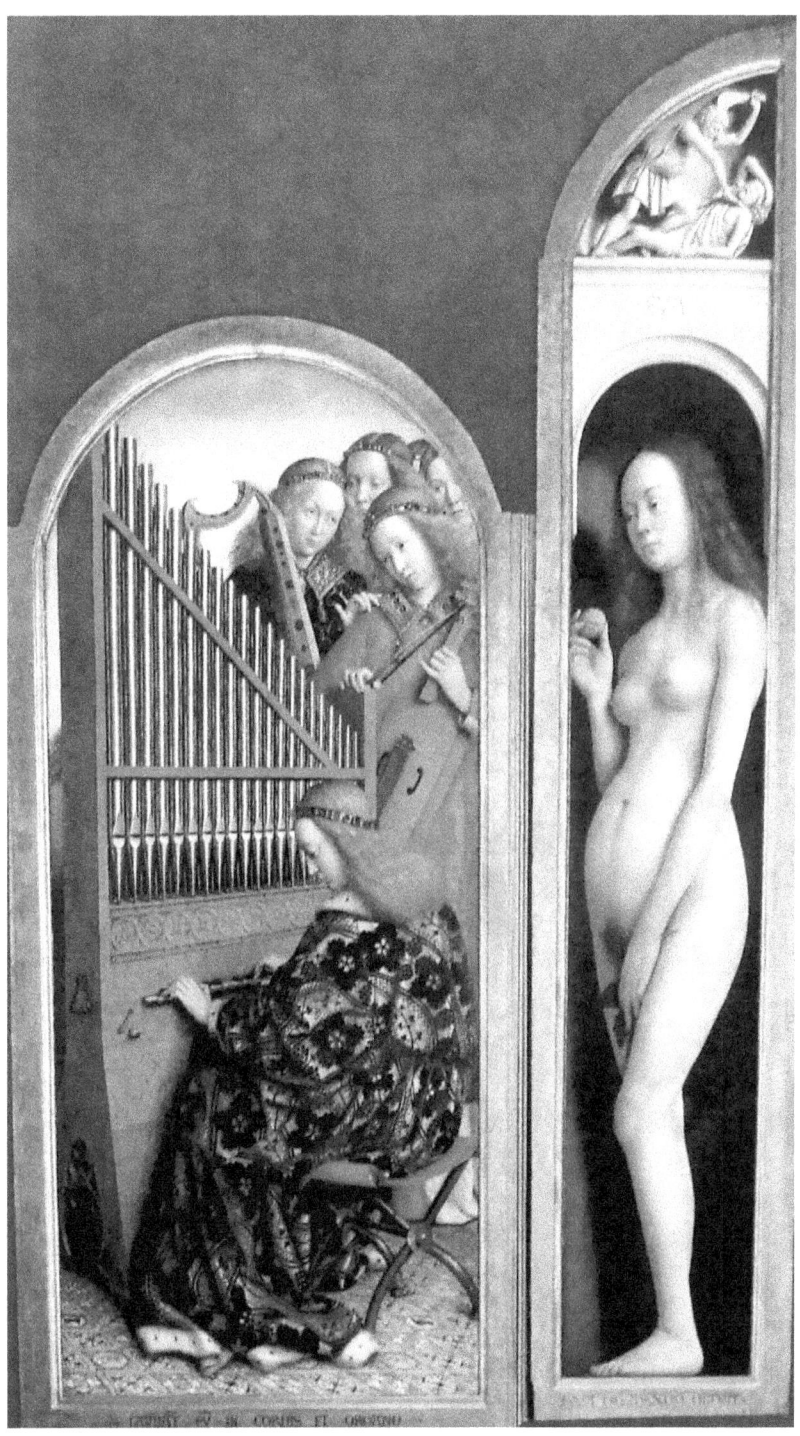

Jan van Eyck, The Ghent Altarpiece, wing

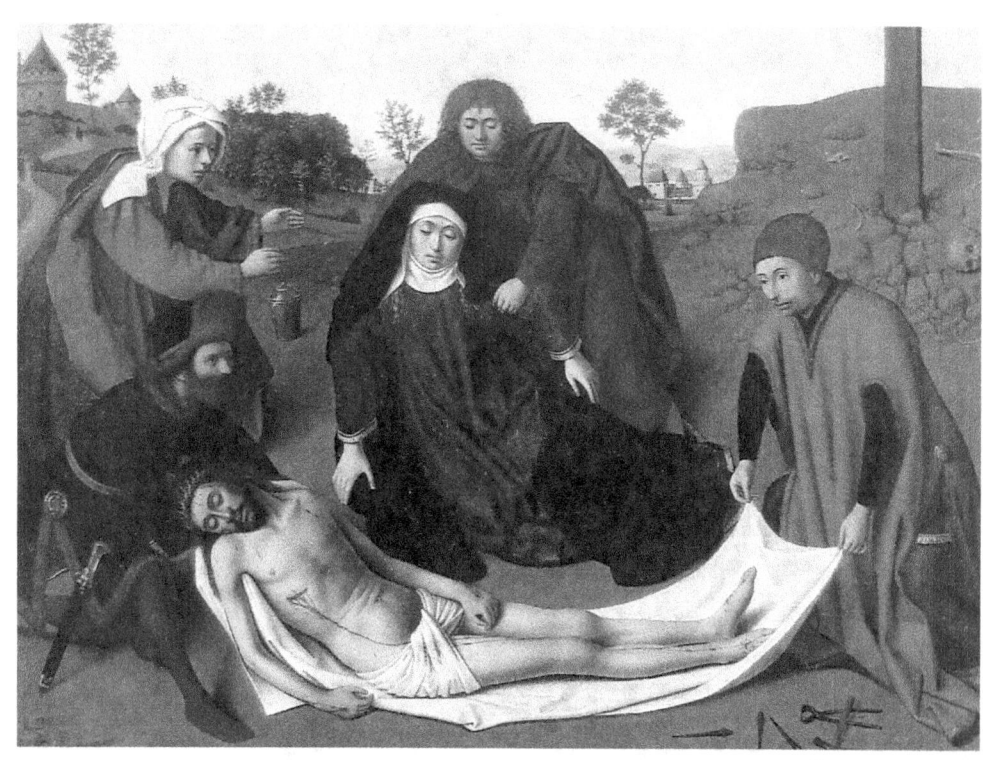

Petrus Christus, The Lamentation, Metropolitan Museum,
New York City

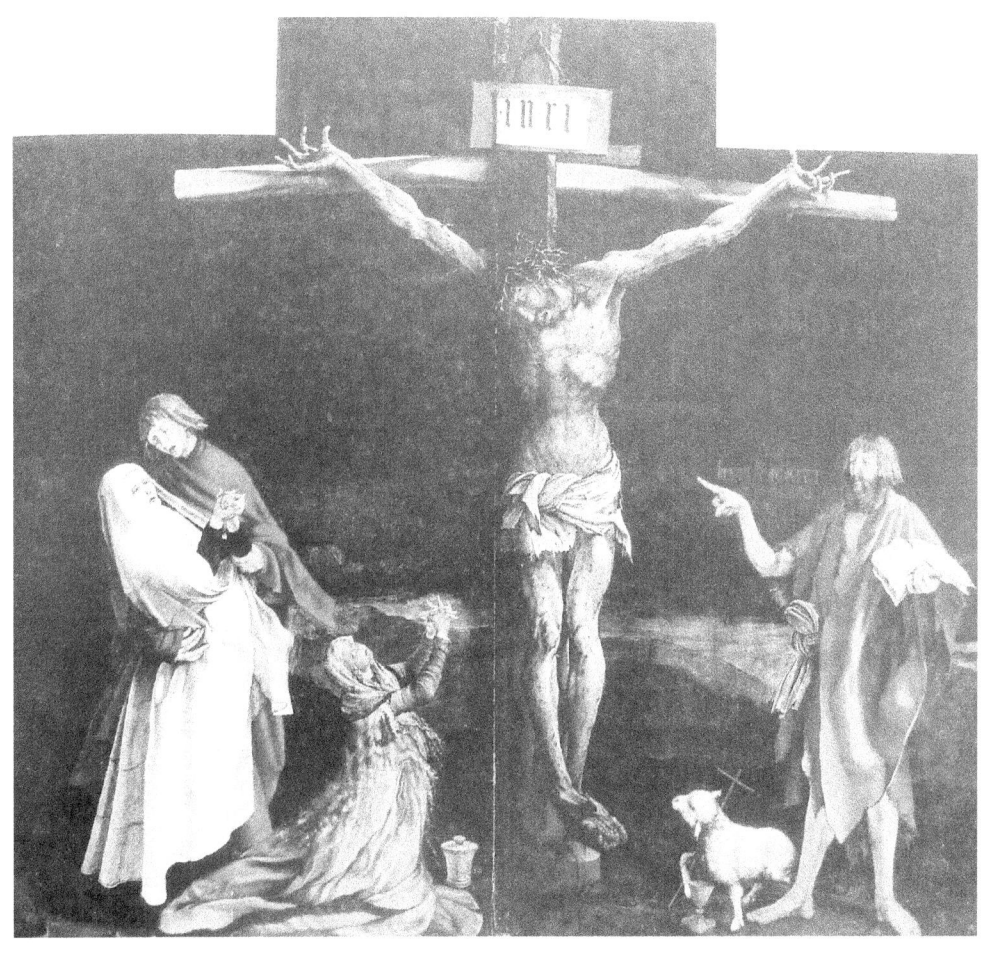

Matthias Grünewald, Crucifixion, Isenheim Altarpiece

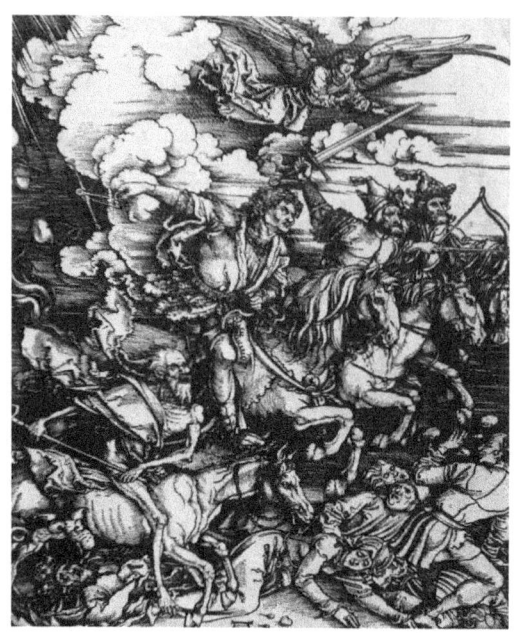

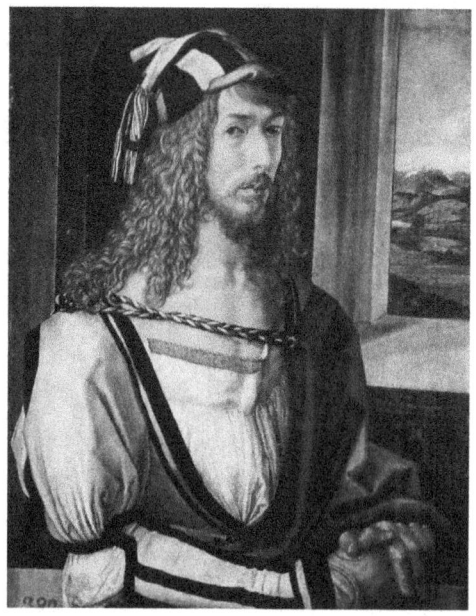

Albrecht Dürer

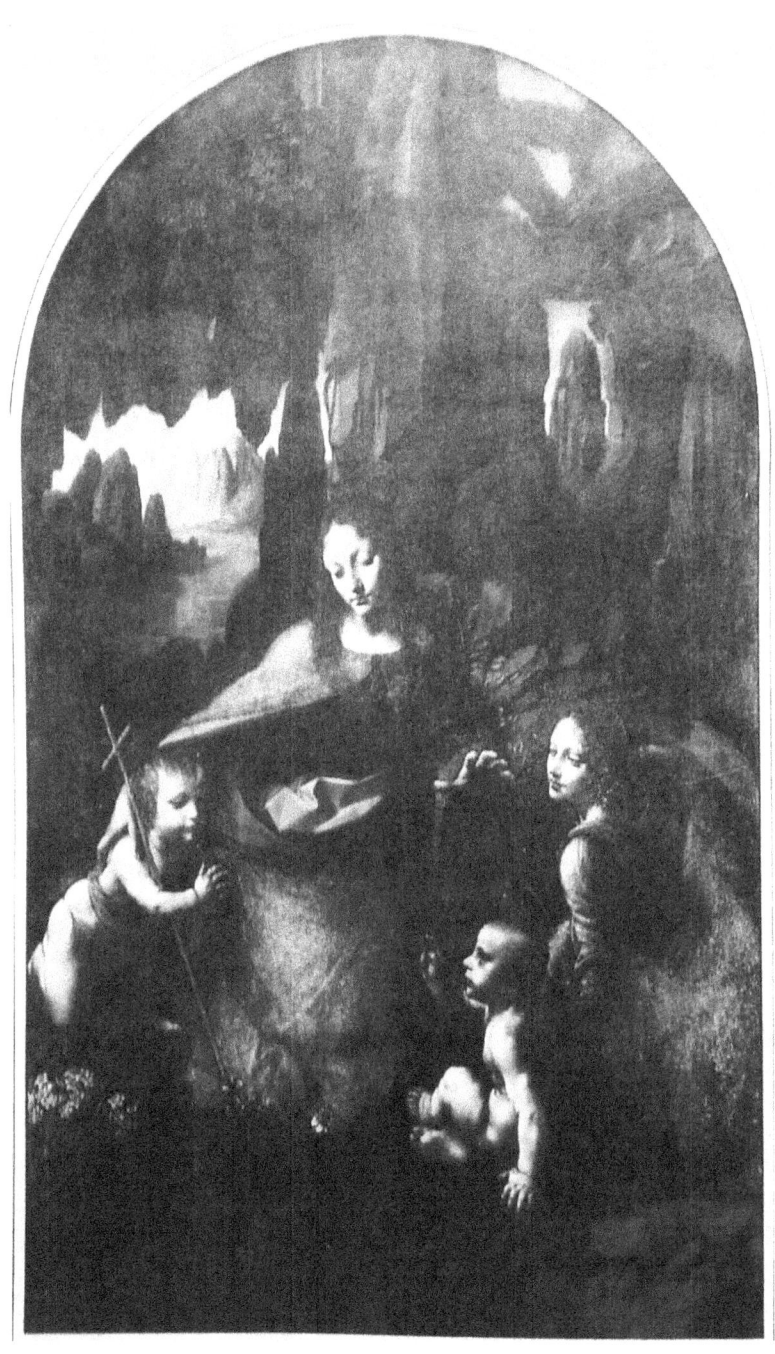

Leonardo da Vinci, The Madonna of the Rocks, London

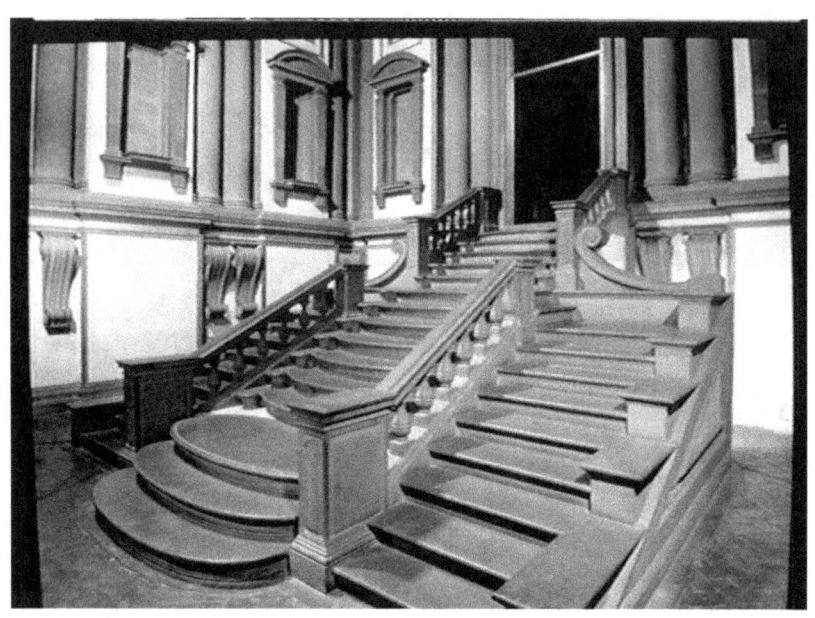

Michelangelo's Medici Library in Firenze. 1524-26
Michelangelo, Mark Rothko said:
'makes the viewers feel that they are trapped in a room where all the
doors and windows are bricked up, so that all they can do is butt their
heads forever against the wall.

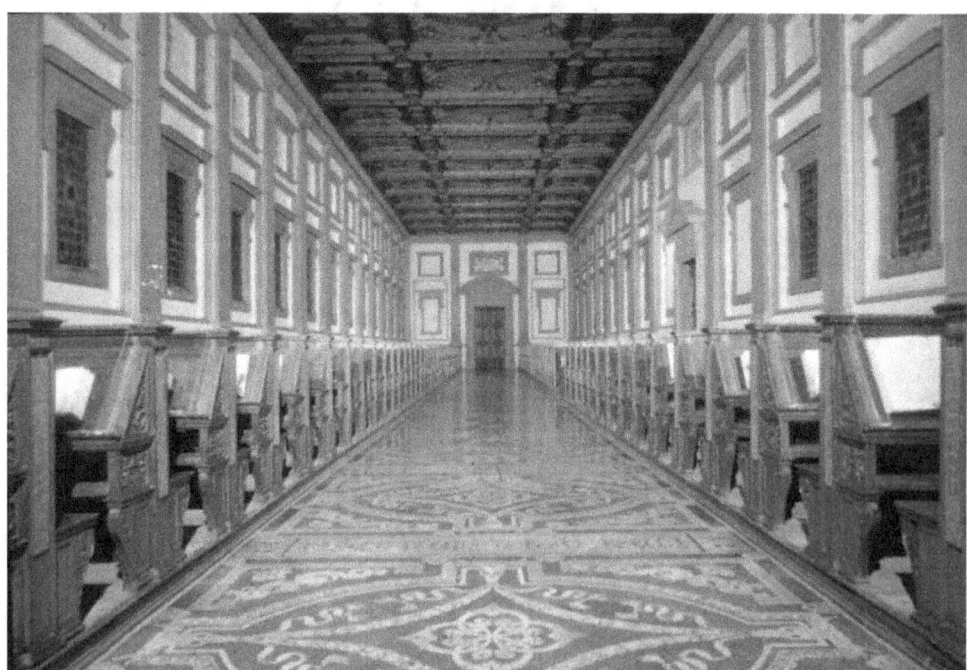

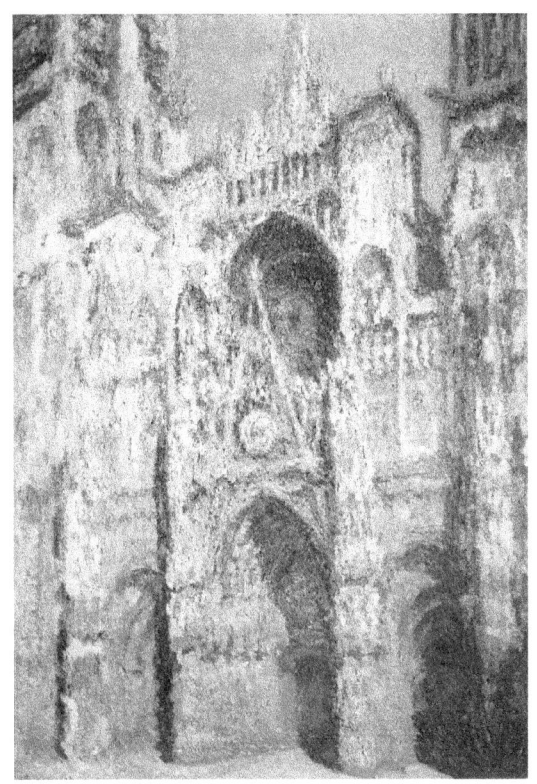

Claude Monet, Rouen Cathedral, above.
Irises in Monet's Garden, 1900, below.

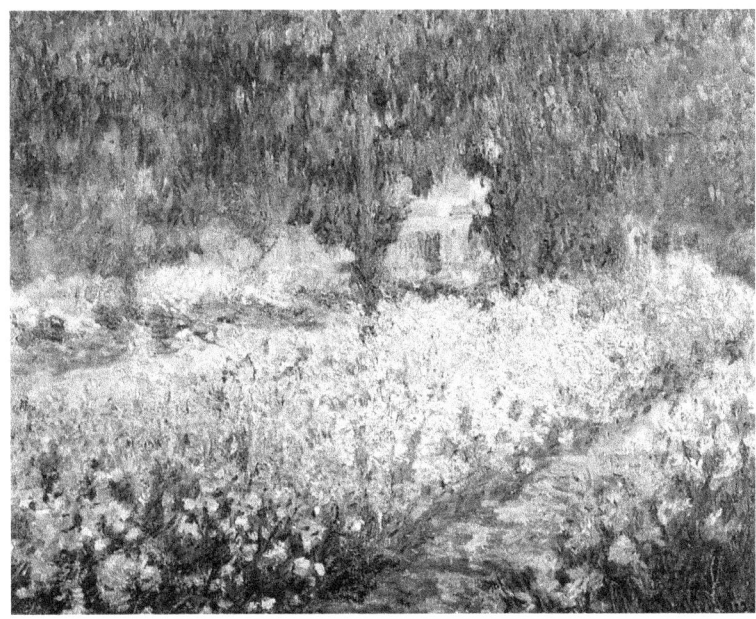

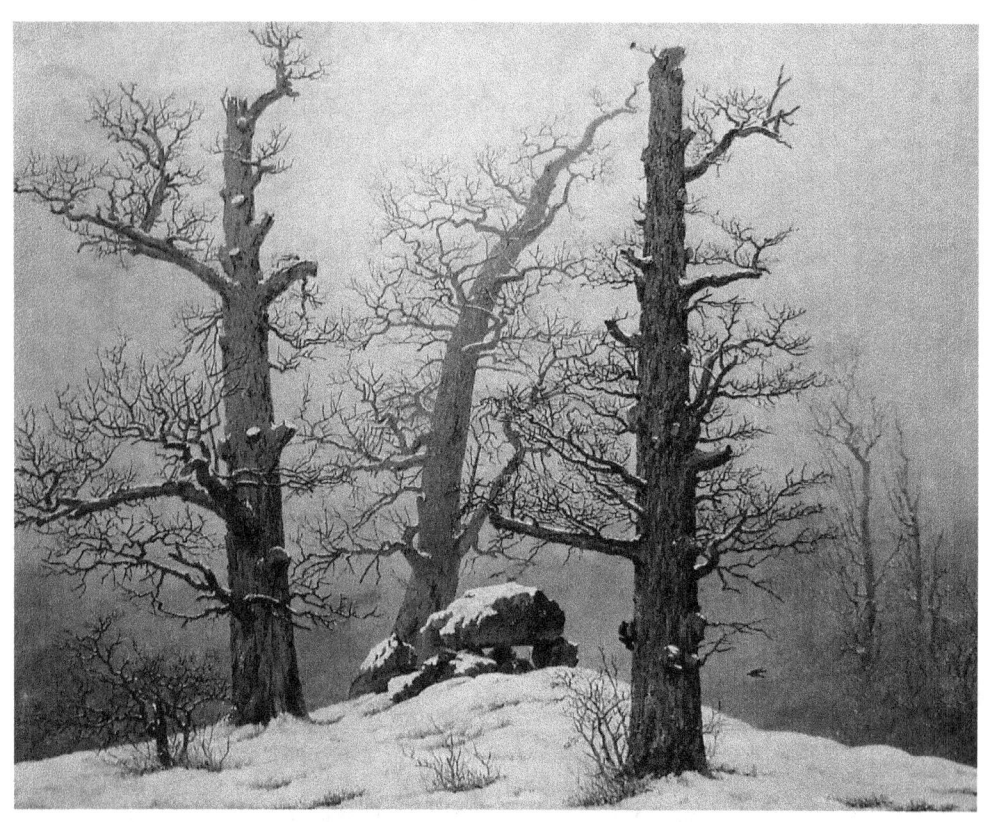

Caspar David Friedrich, Dolmen In the Snow, 1807,
Staatliche Kunstsammlungen, Gemäldesgalerie, Dresden

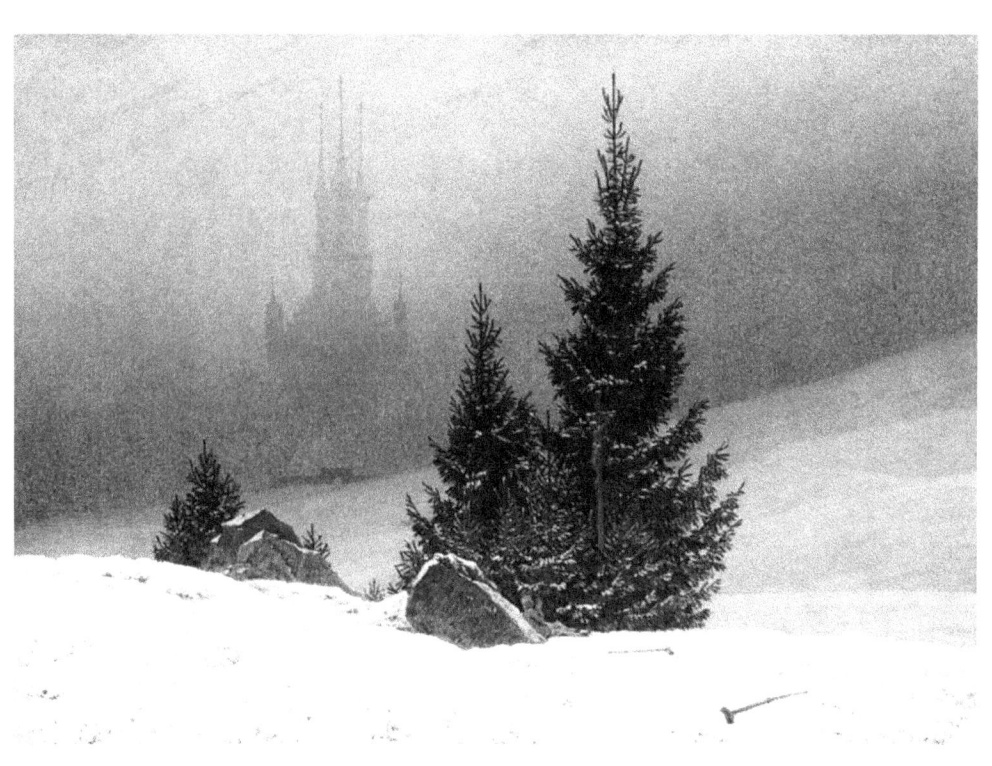

Casper David Friedrich, Winter Landscape, 1811, National Gallery, London

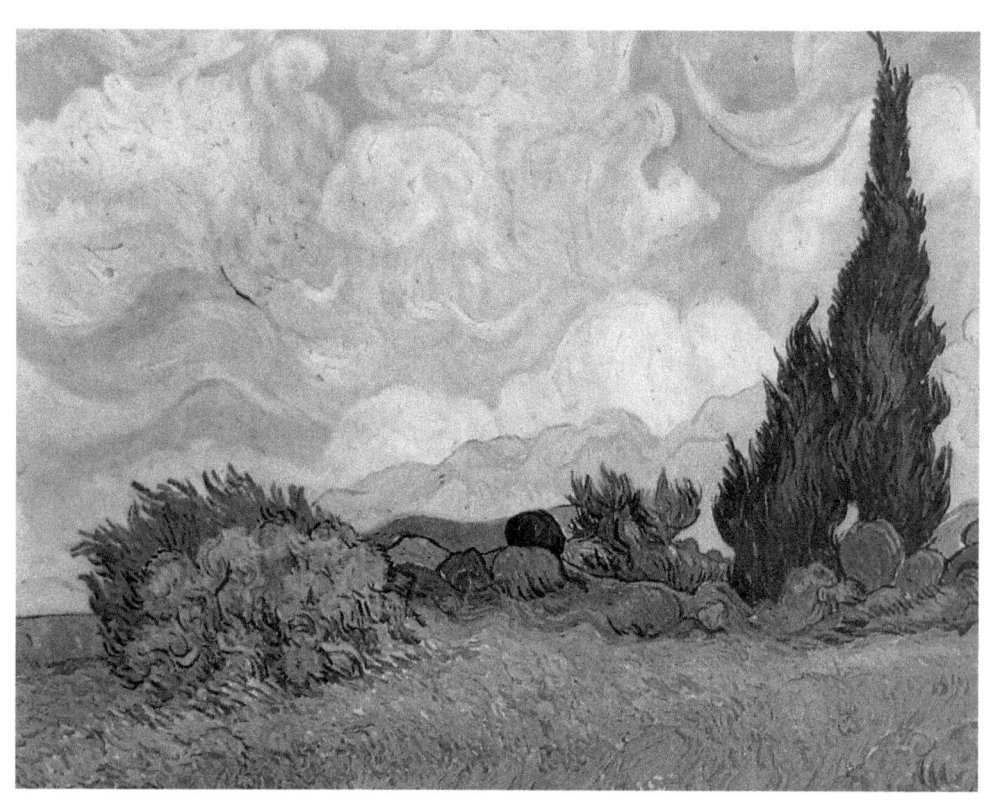

Vincent van Gogh, Wheatfield, Zurich

Kasimir Malevich, Suprematist Composition: White On White, 1918,
Museum of Modern Art, New York

QUOTES BY MARK ROTHKO

Art to me is an anecdote of the spirit, and the only means of making concrete the purpose of its varied quickness and stillness.

•

I also hang the pictures low rather than high, and particularly in the case of the largest ones, often as close to the floor as is feasible, for that is the way they are painted.

•

If our titles recall the known myths of antiquity, we have used them again because they are the eternal symbols upon which we must fall back to express basic psychological ideas.

•

It is a widely accepted notion among painters that it does not matter what one paints as long as it is well painted. This is the essence of academicism.

•

That is why we profess a spiritual kinship with primitive and archaic art.

•

There is no such thing as good painting about nothing.

•

This would be a distortion of their meaning, since the pictures are intimate and intense, and are the opposite of what is decorative; and have been painted in a scale of normal living rather than an institutional scale.

•

We assert that the subject is crucial and only that subject matter is valid which is tragic and timeless.

•

I am not an abstractionist... I am not interested in the relationship of colour or form or anything else... I'm interested only in expressing basic human emotions – tragedy, ecstasy, doom and so on – and the fact that a lot of people break down and cry when confronted with my pictures show that I communicate those basic human emotions... The people who weep before my pictures are having the same religious experience I had when I painted them. And if you, as you say, are moved only by their color relationships, then you miss the point!

•

I will say without reservations that from my view there can be no abstractions. Any shape or area which has not the pulsating concreteness of real flesh and bones, its vulnerability to pleasure or pain is nothing at all. Any picture which does not provide the environment in which the breath of life can be drawn does not interest me.

•

This world of imagination is fancy-free and violently opposed to common sense.

•

I paint very large pictures because I want to create a state of intimacy. A large picture is an immediate transaction. It takes you into it.

•

I quarrel with surrealists and abstract art only as one quarrels with his father and mother.

•

There is a moment of blinding light. There is a moment that seems like death, a paralysis. Then a new man, Paul, emerges from the experience.

•

It is our function as artists to make the spectator see the world our way not his way.

•

I think of my pictures as dramas; the shapes in the pictures are the performers... neither the action, nor the actors can be anticipated or described in advance.

•

We favor the simple expression of complex thought. We are for the large shape because it has the impact of the unequivocal. We wish to reassert the picture plane. We are for flat forms because they destroy illusion and reveal truth.

•

A painting is not about an experience. It is an experience.

•

The myth holds us, therefore, not through its romantic flavor, not the remembrance of beauty of some bygone age, not through the possibilities of fantasy, but because it expresses to us something real and existing in ourselves, as it was to those who first stumbled upon the symbols to give them life.

•

Small pictures since the Renaissance are like novels; large pictures are like dramas in which one participates in a direct way.

•

Since my pictures are large, colorful, and unframed, and since museum walls are usually immense and formidable, there is the danger that the pictures relate themselves as decorative areas to the walls.

•

There will be an exhibition, ... The question is when and how large. It is difficult to convince collectors and museums to send the paintings to Israel. The question of insurance presents difficulties for the project, but we intend to do such an exhibition within two to three years.

•

I have on occasion successfully dealt with this problem by tending to crowd the show rather than making it spare.

It is really a matter of ending this silence and solitude, of breathing and stretching one's arms again.

·

When I was a younger man, art was a lonely thing. No galleries, no collectors, no critics, no money. Yet, it was a golden age, for we all had nothing to lose and a vision to gain. Today it is not quite the same. It is a time of tons of verbiage, activity, consumption. Which condition is better for the world at large I shall not venture to discuss. But I do know, that many of those who are driven to this life are desperately searching for those pockets of silence where we can root and grow. We must all hope we find them.

·

A picture lives by companionship, expanding and quickening in the eyes of the sensitive observer. It dies by the same token. It is therefore risky to send it out into the world. How often it must be impaired by the eyes of the unfeeling and the cruelty of the impotent.

·

It was with the utmost reluctance that I found the figure could not serve my purposes. But a time came when none of us could use the figure without mutilating it.

·

The progression of a painter's work as it travels in time from point to point, will be toward clarity... toward the elimination of all obstacles between the painter and the idea... and the idea and the observer... To achieve this clarity is inevitably to be understood.

·

I seem to have to do it elaborately wrong and with many conceits first. Then maybe I can attack and deflate my pomposity and arrive at something straight and simple.

·

If what a person makes is completely and profoundly right according to his lights then this work contains the whole man. A work which falls short of this content, is only of passing value and lends itself to arbitrariness and fragmentation.

•

Silence is so accurate.

NOTES

I *Introduction: A Vertical Portrait of the Artist*

1. E. Carr, in M. Witzling, 179.
2. M. Rothko, 1987, 24f; R. Rosenblum, 1978.
3. R. Rosenblum, *Art News*, 59, 10, Feb, 1961.
4. See D. Ashton; D. Waldman.

II *Mark Rothko Criticism*

1. D. Ashton, 1958; A. Brookner: "The New New York Scene", *Burlington Magazine*, 103, Nov, 1963; B. Robertson, 1961; M. Kozloff, 1961; R. Hobbs, 1978; D. Waldman, 1978, 69; P. Selz, in R. Goldwater; R. Goldwater, 1961; C. Greenberg, 1955, 193; D. Sylvester, 1961; I. Sandler, 1983; W. de Kooning, 1958, 176.
2. J. Ashbery, "Paris Notes", *Art International*, Feb 25, 1963, 73.
3. R. Motherwell, in E. de Antonio, 65.
4. T. Matthews, "The Problem of Religious Content in Contemporary Art", lecture, Congress on Religion, Architecture and the Visual Arts, New York, NY, 1967.
5. Robert Hughes reckons that Mark Rothko may have been a religious painter, but in another era (1978b, 16).
6. M. Heidegger, *Der Satz vom Grund*, Pfullingen, Neske, 1957.
7. M. Foucault, *The Order of Things*, Tavistock, 1970.
8. F. Jameson, "Postmodernism, or the Cultural Logic of Late Capitalism", *New Left Review*, 146, Aug, 1984, 83.
9. J. Baudrillard, *America*, Verso, London, 1988.
10. J. Baudrillard, ib., 71.
11. R. Braidotti, *Patterns of Dissonance*, Polity Press, London, 1991, 14.
12. J. Derrida, *Psyché: inventions de l'autre*, Galilée, Paris, 1987, 562.
13. J. Kristeva, *Revolution in Poetic Language*, Columbia University Press,

New York, NY, 1984.

14. J. Kristeva, "Jackson Pollock's Milky Way, 1912-56", *Journal of Philosophy and the Visual Arts*, 1, 1989, 34-39.
15. D. Ashton, "Art", *Arts and Architecture*, Apl, 1 958.
16. J. Reed, *Lipstick, Sex and Poetry*, Peter Owen, London, 1991, 108.
17. G. Auty in "Romantically Inclined", in A.C. Papadakis, *The New Romantics*, 62.

III *The American Renaissance: Mark Rothko and Abstract Expressionism*

1. R. Motherwell, address to the National Institute of Arts and Letters, Jan, 1971.
2. B. Newman, in E. de Antonio, 43.
3. F. Jameson, "Postmodernism and consumer society", in H. Foster, 111.
4. On Barnett Newman see K. Baker, 1980; Y.-A. Bois, "Perceiving Newman", *Painting as Model*, MIT Press, Cambridge, MA, 1990; A. Gibson; M. Kimmelman, "Newman's Quest for a Vocabulary", *The New York Times*, Apl 15, 1988; J.B. Klaster, "Red Alert", *Artnews*, 91, 2, Feb, 1992; M. Zakian: "Barnett Newman and the Sublime", *Arts Magazine*, 62, 6, Feb, 1988, and "Barnett Newman: Painting a Sense of Place", *Arts Magazine*, 62, 7, Mch, 1988.
On Barnett Newman and the 'Abstract Sublime', see B. Cavaliere, "Barnett Newman's *Vir Heroicus Sublimis*: Building the 'Idea Complex'", *Arts Magazine*, 55, 5, Jan, 1981; I. Dunlop; P. Crowther, "Barnett Newman and the Sublime", *Oxford Art Journal*, 7, 2, 1984; D. J. Glaser, "Transcendence in the Vision of Barnett Newman", *The Journal of Aesthetics and Art Criticism*, 40, 4, Summer, 1982; R. Nikas, "The Sublime Was Then (Search for Tomorrow", *Arts Magazine*, 60, 7, Mch, 1986; P. Taaffe, "Sublimity, Now and Forever, Amen", *Arts Magazine*, 60, 7, Mch, 1986; L. Alloway, "The Stations of the Cross and the Subjects of the Artist", in *Barnett Newman: The Stations of the Cross: Lama Sabacthani*, Guggenheim Museum, 1966; H. Rosenberg, 1975.
5. See D. Davis, "The Red, the Yellow, the Blue", *Newsweek*, Oct 18, 1971; T. de Duve, "Who's Afraid of Red, Yellow, and Blue?", *Artforum*, 22, 1, Sept, 1983; M. Imdahl, *Barnett Newman: Who's Afraid of Red, Yellow and Blue III*, Werkmonographien zur Bildenden Kunst, 147, 1971.
6. H. Rosenberg, 1971.
7. P. Heron, quoted in P. Fuller, "Patrick Heron: The Innocent Eye?", *Artscribe*, 51, June, 1985, and in P. Fuller, 1993, 220-1.
8. P. Heron, 1973, in P. Fuller, 1993, 221.
9. P. Fuller, "St Ives", *Artscribe*, 53, June, 1985; and see P. Fuller: "The Legacy of Mark Rothko", *Art Monthly*, 20, Oct, 1978.
10. P. Fuller, 1993, 217.

`11. M. Rothko, in 1960, quoted in G. Drudi, in D. Ashton, 1983, 187.

IV *Mark Rothko's Aesthetics*

1. Peter Selz offers a typical critical view of Rothko's art as an apparently serene surface masking inner, Nietzschean turmoil:

   An Apollonian intensity becomes evident in Rothko's work once we go beyond the immediate sensual appeal of the beautiful color relationships... his work does not so much resolve agitation as contain it, in the sense of holding it within bounds. These apparently quiet, contemplative surfaces are only masks for underlying turmoil and passion. (P. Selz, "Mark Rothko", in B. Robertson, 18).

2. Arshile Gorky wrote: 'Art must be serious, no sarcasm, no comedy. One does not laugh at a loved one.' "Jan 17, 1947", *Ararat*, 12, Fall, 1944.
3. Pratt Institute lecture notes, in D. Ashton, *The New York Times*, Oct 31, 1958.
4. 'I do not believe that there was ever a question of being abstract or representational. It is really a matter of ending this silence and solitude, of breathing and stretching one's arms again', said Rothko (1947-48).
5. L. Lippard, "Escalataion in Washington", *Art International*, 12, 1, Jan, 1968, 42.
6. M. Kozloff, "A Letter to the Editor", *Art International*, 7, 6, June, 1963, 90.

V *Mark Rothko's 'Multiform' Paintings of the 1940s-1960s*

1. M. Rothko, in Janis, 118.
2. See L. Alloway, "The American Sublime", *Living Arts*, June, 1963.
3. H. Crehan, "Rothko's Wall of Light: A Show of His New Work at Chicago", *Arts Digest*, 1, 1954, 19.
4. M. Rothko, *Time*, Mch 3, 1961.

VI *Sacred Spaces: The Rothko Chapels and Murals*

1. There has been much critical attention focussed on the Houston Chapel. For example, J.-P. Marandel, "Une chapelle oecuménique au Texas", *L'Oeil*, 197, May, 1971; D. Menil, "The Rothko Chapel", *Art Journal*, 30, 3, Spring, 1971; D. Ashton, "The Rothko Chapel in Houston", *Studio*, 181, 934, June, 1971; B. O'Doherty, "The Rothko Chapel", *Art in*

America, 61, 1, Jan, 1973; A. Holmes, "The Rothko Chapel Six Years Later", *Art News*, 73, 10, Dec, 1976; C.R. Cernuschi, "Mark Rothko's mature paintings", *Arts Magazine*, May, 1986; Rothko, 1978; R. Hughes' *Shock of the New*, BBC, London, 1981; S. Barnes, "The Making of the Chapel: *Broken Obelisk*", in *The Rothko Chapel,* 1989.

2. See T. Hess, "Barnett Newman: Stations of the Cross — Lema Sabachthani", *American Art at Mid-Century*, National Gallery, Washington, DC, 1978; J. Dillenberger, "*The Stations of the Cross* by Barnett Newman", *Secular Art with Sacred Themes*, Abingdon Press, New York, NY, 1969; E. Genauer, "Christ's Journey on Canvas", *New York Herald Tribune*, Apl 20, 1966; L. Alloway, "Color, Culture, The Stations: Notes on the Barnett Newman Memorial Exhibition", *Artforum*, 10, 4, Dec, 1971; J. Masheck, "Cruciformality", *Artforum*, 15, 10, Summer, 1977; H. Rosenberg 1978; I. Sandler, 1970.

3. Newman, quoted in Rosenberg, 1978, 77. Barnett Newman: *Broken Obelisk*, 1963-67, Cor-Ten steel, 26 ft high, Institute of Religion and Human Development, Houston, TX.

4. E.C. Goossen: "The Philosophic Line of B. Newman", *Art News*, Summer 1958; Harold Rosenberg: *Art on the Edge*, Macmillan, 1975. On Brancusi, see E. Shanes: *Constantin Brancusi*, Abbeville, New York, NY, 1989

5. M. Rothko, quoted by Robert Motherwell in 1967, in D. Ashton, 1983, 174.

6. A. Reinhardt, interview, *Art International*, Dec, 1966, 18f.

7. A. Reinhardt, 1991, 10.

8. R. Stankiewicz, *Sixteen Americans*, MOMA, New York, NY, 1959.

9. B. Newman, in H. Rosenberg, 1994, 59.

10. M. Rothko, in D. Ashton, 1983, 179. Ad Reinhardt was less generous about Mark Rothko. In some undated notes, Reinhardt wrote:

What's wrong with the art world is not Andy Andy Warhol or Andy Wyeth but Mark Rothko. The corruption of the best is the worst. Motherwell said someone said, "Rothko is the best Jewish artist in the world." ... How about Christians making synagogue murals? (Motherwell). How about Jews decorating Catholic churches? (Rothko). (1991, 190).

11. T. Merton, *Seeds of Contemplation*, Burns & Oates, London, 1962, 196.

12. P. Tillich, "Art", *Newsweek*, Feb, 1959, 54.

13. R. Motherwell in R. Hobbs, 1978; B. O'Doherty, 1973.

14. So used are viewers to the notion and experience of a Mark Rothko Room or 'chapel', it is odd to think of Rothko's Seagram murals hanging on the walls of the Four Seasons Restaurant. Rothko himself said he did not wish his paintings to serve as a background to the meals

of the privileged. (See J. Fisher, "The Easy Chair", *Harper's Magazine*, July, 1970).

15. D. Ashton, 1983, 147.

VI *The Late Grey, Brown and Black Works*

1. D. Ashton, 1983, 188.

BIBLIOGRAPHY

MARK ROTHKO

Mark Rothko 1903-1970: A Retrospective, Guggenheim, New York, NY 1978

Mark Rothko: The 1958-59 Murals, Pace Gallery, New York, NY, 1978

Mark Rothko: Seven Paintings From the 1960s, text by Bonnie Clearwater, Walker Arts Center, Minneapolis, 1983

Mark Rothko: Paintings 1948-1969, text by Irving Sandler, Pace Gallery, New York, NY, 1983

Mark Rothko: Works on Paper, National Gallery of Art, Washington, 1984

Mark Rothko: Subjects, text Anna Chave, High Museum of Art, Atlanta, 1984

Mark Rothko: The Dark Paintings 1969-70, Pace Gallery, New York, NY, 1985

Mark Rothko, 1903-1970, Tate Gallery, London, 1987

Mark Rothko & Miguel Lopez-Remiro. *Writings on Art*, 2006

letter to Edward Alden Jewel, *New York Times*, 13 June, 1943

"The Portrait and the Modern Artist", TS, "Art in New York", Radio WNYC, 13 October, 1943

"Personal Statement", David Porter Gallery, Washington, 1945

["The romantics were prompted"], *Possibilities*, no. 1, Winter, 1947-48

statement, *Tiger's Eye,* no. 9, October, 1949

interview, *Interiors*, 10 May, 1951

interview, in W. Seitz, 1952

Pratt Institute lectures, notes, in Dore Ashton's article in *Cimaise*, December, 1958

notes for the 1961 Whitechapel exhibition, London, 1961

SOURCES

David Anfam: *Abstract Expressionism*, Thames & Hudson, London, 1990

Emile de Antonio & Mitch Tuchman: *Painters Painting*, Abbeville Press, New York, NY, 1984

H.H. Arnason: *Robert Motherwell*, Abrams, New York, NY, 1982

Dore Ashton: *American Art Since 1945*, Thomas & Hudson, London, 1982

— *About Rothko*, Oxford University Press, New York, NY, 1983

— "Rothko's Passion", *Art International*, Feb, 1979

— "Art: Mark Rothko", *Arts & Architecture*, vol. 75, April, 1958

Michael Auping. *Declaring Space: Mark Rothko, Barnett Newman, Lucio Fontana, Yves Klein*, 2007

K. Baker: "Reckoning with Notation: The Drawings of Pollock, Newman, and Louis", *Artforum*, 18, no. 10, Summer, 1980

Gregory Battock, ed. *Minimal Art: A Critical Anthology*, Studio Vista, 1969

Maurice Berger: *Labyrinths: Robert Morris, Minimalism and the 1960s*, Harper & Row, New York, NY, 1989

Georges Boudaille: *Expressionists*, Alpine Fine Arts Collection, London, 1976

Helmut Brinker: *Zen in the Art of Painting*, Routledge & Kegan Paul, London, 1987

Nicolas & Elena Calas: *Icons and Image of the Sixties*, Dutton, New York, NY, 1971

Joseph Campbell: *The Power of Myth*, with Bill Moyers, ed. Betty Sue Flowers, Doubleday, New York, NY, 1988

Barbara Cavaliere: "Notes on Rothko", *Flash Art*, nos. 86-87, Jan, 1979

Herschel B. Chipp, ed. *Theories of Modern Art*, University Press of California, Los Angeles, 1968

Bonnie Clearwater: *Mark Rothko: Works on Paper*, National Gallery of Art, Washington, 1984

— "How Rothko Looked at Rothko", *Art News*, November, 1985

— *The Rothko Book: Tate Essential Artists Series*, Tate, London, 2007

— & Dore Ashton. *Mark Rothko: Works on Paper*, 2008

Marjorie B. Cohn. *Mark Rothko*, 2005

Frances Colpitt: *Minimal Art: The Critical Perspective*, University of Washington Press, Seattle, 1990

John Coplans: "Post-Painterly Abstraction", *Artforum*, vol.2, no.12, Summer, 1964, 4-9

— "Serial Imagery", *Artforum*, vol.7, no. 2, October, 1968, 34-43

Joseph Cornell: *Theatre of the Mind: Selected Diaries, Letters, and Files*, ed. Mary Ann Caws, Thames & Hudson, London, 1993

Michael Crichton: *Jasper Johns*, Thames & Hudson, London, 1977

Jean-Luc Daval: *History of Abstract Painting*, Art Data, London, 1989

Elaine de Kooning: "Kline and Rothko: Two Americans in Action", *Art News Annual*, no. 27, 1958

Willis Domingo: "The Intuition of Form", *Arts Magazine*, 47, no. 4, Feb, 1973

Wolf-Dieter Dube: *The Expressionists*, Thames & Hudson, London, 1972

Ian Dunlop: "Edvard Munch, Barnett Newman and Mark Rothko: The Search For the Sublime", *Arts Magazine*, Feb, 1979

John Elderfield: *Helen Frankenthaler*, New York, NY, 1989

Mircea Eliade: *Ordeal by Labyrinth*, University of Chicago Press, 1984

— *Symbolism, the Sacred and the Arts*, Crossroad, New York, NY, 1985

Eve Firestone: "Color in Abstract Expressionism: Sources and Background For Meaning", *Arts Magazine*, March, 1981

John Fischer: "The Easy Chair: Mark Rothko: portrait of the artist as an augury man", *Harper's*, vol. 241, no. 1442, July, 1970

Hal Foster, ed. *The Anti-Aesthetic: Essays in Postmodern Culture*, Bay Press, Port Townsend, 1983

Richard Francis: *Jasper Johns,* New York, NY, 1984

E. Franz: *Jackson Pollock*, Abbeville, New York, NY, 1983

Michael Fried: *Three American Painters: Kenneth Noland, Jules Olitski, Frank Stella*, Fogg Art Museum, Harvard University, Cambridge, Mass., 1965

— "Art and Objecthood", *Artforum*, 5, Summer 1967, 12-23

— "Shape as Form: Frank Stella's New Paintings", *Artforum*, vol.5, no.3, November, 1966

— *Morris Louis*, Abrams, New York, NY, 1970

Peter Fuller: *Peter Fuller's Modern Painters: Reflections on British Art*, ed. John McDonald, Methuen, London, 1993

Ann Gibson: "Regression and Color in Abstract Expressionism: Barnett Newman, Mark Rothko and Clyfford Still", *Arts Magazine*, March, 1981

Bruce Glaser: "Questions to Stella and Judd", ed. Lucy Lippard, *Art News*, vol. 65, no.5, September, 1966, 55-61

Donald Goddard: "Rothko's Journey Into the Unknown", *Art News*, vol. 78, no. 1, Jan, 1979

Robert Goldwater: "Reflections on the Rothko Exhibition", *Arts Magazine*, vol. 35, no. 6, March, 1961

— & Marco Treves, eds. *Artists on Art*, John Murray, London, 1975

Clement Greenberg: "American-Type Painting", *Partisan Review*, Spring, 1955

— "Modernist Painting", *Arts Yearbook*, 4, Art Digest, New York, NY, 1961, 100-8

— *Post-Painterly Abstraction*, Los Angeles County Museum, Los Angeles, 1964

Thomas Hess: *Barnett Newman*, Walker, New York, NY, 1969

Robert Hewison: *Future Tense: A New Art For the Nineties*, Methuen, London, 1990

Robert Carleton Hobbs & Gail Levin: *Abstract Expressionism: The Formative Years*, Whitney Museum of American Art, 1978

Friedrich Hölderlin. *Poems and Fragments*, tr. M. Hamburger, Anvil Press, 1994

Sam Hunter, ed. *An American Renaissance: Painting and Sculpture Since 1940*, Abbeville Press, New York, NY, 1986

— *American Art of the 20th Century*, Thames & Hudson, London, 1973

Sidney Janis: *Abstract and Surrealist Art in America*, New York, NY, 1944

C.G. Jung: *Memories, Dreams, Reflections*, Collins, London, 1967

Max Kozloff: *Jasper Johns*, New York, NY, 1969

— "Mark Rothko's New Retrospective", *Art Journal*, vol. 20, no. 3, 1961

Julia Kristeva: *The Kristeva Reader*, ed. Toril Moi, Blackwell, London, 1986

— *Desire in Language: A Semiotic Approach to Literature and Art*, ed. Leon Roudiez, tr. Thomas Gora, Alice Jardine & Leon Roudiez, Blackwell, 1982

Lucy Lippard: *From the Center: feminist essays on women's art*, Dutton, New York, NY, 1976

— *Ad Reinhardt*, Abrahams, New York, NY, 1981

— *Six Years: The Dematerialization of the Art Object from 1966 to 1972*, Praeger, New York, NY, 1973

Donald McKinney: *Mark Rothko*, Kunsthaus Zürich, 1971

Dorothy C. Miller, ed. *Sixteen Americans*, MOMA, New York, NY, 1959

Catherine Millett: "De Kooning, Newman, Rothko: des bâtards", *Art Press International*, no. 26, March, 1979

Anna Moszynska: *Abstract Art*, Thames & Hudson, London, 1990

Barnett Newman: *Selected Writings and Interviews*, ed. J.P. O'Neill, Knopf, New York, NY, 1990

— *The Stations of the Cross*, Guggenheim, New York, NY, 66

— "The 14 Stations of the Cross", *Artnews*, 65, no. 3, May 1966

Friedrich Nietzsche: *Beyond Good and Evil*, Allen & Unwin, London, 1923

Sheldon Nodelman: *Marden, Novros, Rothko: Painting in the Age of Actuality*, Institute for the Arts, Rice University, Houston, 1978

Klaus Ottmann. *The Essential Mark Rothko*, 2003

Rudolf Otto: *The Idea of the Holy*, Oxford University Press, London, 1958

Michael Payne: *Reading Theory: An Introduction to Lacan, Derrida, and Kristeva*, Blackwell, London, 1993

Robert Payne: *Leonardo da Vinci*, Robert Hale 1979

Guido Perocco: *Mark Rothko*, Museo d'Arte Moderno Ca'Pesaro, Venice, 1970

Michael Phillipson: *Painting, Language and Modernity*, Routledge, London, 1978

Carter Ratcliff: *In the Realm of the Monochrome*, Renaissance Society, University of Chicago, Chicago, 1979

—"Mostly Monochrome", *Art in America*, vol. 69, no.4, April 1981, 111-131

Kathleen J. Reiger, ed. *The Spiritual Image in Modern Art*, Theosophical Publishing House, Wheaton, Illinois, 1987

Ad Reinhardt: *Art as Art: The Selected Writings of Ad Reinhardt*, University of California Press, Berkeley, 1991

Andrew C. Ritche: *Salute to Mark Rothko*, Yale University Art Gallery, New Haven, 1971

Bryan Robertson, ed. *Mark Rothko: A Retrospective Exhibition, Paintings 1945-1960*, Whitechapel, London, 1961

Corinne Robins, ed. *The Pluralist Era: American Art 1968-1981*, Harper & Row, New York, NY, 1984

Barbara Rose: *American Art Since 1900*, Thames & Hudson, London, 1967

—*American Painting*, Skira/ Rizzoli International, New York, NY, 1986

Harold Rosenberg, *The Tradition of the New*, Da Capo Press, New York, NY, 1994

—*The De-Definition of Art*, University of Chicago Press, 1972

Robert Rosenblum: *Modern Painting and the Northern Romantic Tradition*, Thames & Hudson, London, 1978

—*Mark Rothko*, Pace Gallery, New York, NY, 1981

Stephanie Rosenthal. *Black Paintings: Robert Rauschenberg, Ad Reinhardt, Mark Rothko, Frank Stella*, 2007

Christopher Rothko & Kate Prizel Rothko. *The Artist's Reality: Philosophies of Art by Mark Rothko*, 2006

Irwin Sandler: *The Triumph of American Painting*, Harper & Row 1970

—*American Art of the 1960s*, Harper & Row, New York, 1988

—"The New Cool-Art", *Art in America*, vol. 53, vol. 1, Feb, 1965, 97

—in M. Rothko, 1983

Peter Schjeldahl: *Art in Our Time: The Saatchi Collection*, Lund Humphries, 1984

—"Rothko and Belief", *Art in America*, March, 1979

Barry Schwabsky: "The Real Situation: Philip Guston and Mark Rothko at the End of the Sixties", *Arts Magazine*, vol. 61, no. 4, December, 1986

William Seitz: interview with Mark Rothko, 22 Jan, 1952

Lee Seldes: *The Legacy of Mark Rothko*, Secker & Warburg, London, 1978

Peter Selz: *Mark Rothko*, MOMA, New York, NY, 1961

David Shapiro & Cecil Shapiro, eds. *Abstract Expressionism: A Critical Record*, Cambridge University Press, 1990

David Smith: *Sculpture and Drawings*, ed. Jörn Merkert, Prestel-Verlag, Munich, 1981

Naomi Spector: *Robert Ryman*, Whitechapel Art Gallery, London, 1977

Nikos Stangos, ed. *Concepts of Modern Art*, Thames & Hudson, London,

1981

Frank Stella: *Working Space*, Harvard University Press, Cambridge, Mass., 1986

David Sylvester: "Rothko", *New Statesman*, 20 October, 1961

Jacob Baal-Teshuva. *Mark Rothko*, Taschen, 2009

Maurice Tuchman: *The New York School*, Thames & Hudson, London, 1971

—*The Spiritual in Art: Abstract Painting 1880-1985*, Los Angeles County Museum of Art/ Abbeville Press, New York, NY, 1986

Paul Vogt: *Contemporary Painting*, Abrahams, New York, NY, 1981

Diane Waldman: *Mark Rothko*, Thames & Hudson, London, 1978

Daniel Wheeler: *Art Since Mid-Century: 1945 to the Present*, Thames & Hudson, London, 1991

John White: *The Birth and Rebirth of Pictorial Space*, Faber, London, 1957/87

Marion Whybrow: *St Ives 1883-1993: Portrait of an Art Colony*, Antique Collector's Club, London, 1994

Oliver Wick & Katy Spurrell. *Mark Rothko*, 2008

Mara R. Witzling, ed. *Voicing Our Visions: Writings by Women Artists*, Women's Press, London, 1992

Gerard Woods *et al*, eds. *Art Without Boundaries*, Thames & Hudson, London, 1972

CRESCENT MOON PUBLISHING

web: www.crmoon.com e-mail: cresmopub@yahoo.co.uk

ARTS, PAINTING, SCULPTURE

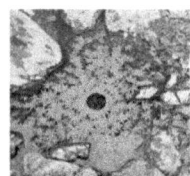

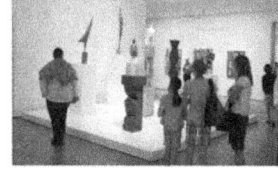

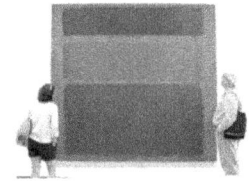

The Art of Andy Goldsworthy
Andy Goldsworthy: Touching Nature
Andy Goldsworthy in Close-Up
Andy Goldsworthy: Pocket Guide
Andy Goldsworthy In America
Land Art: A Complete Guide
The Art of Richard Long
Richard Long: Pocket Guide
Land Art In the UK
Land Art in Close-Up
Land Art In the U.S.A.
Land Art: Pocket Guide
Installation Art in Close-Up
Minimal Art and Artists In the 1960s and After
Colourfield Painting
Land Art DVD, TV documentary
Andy Goldsworthy DVD, TV documentary
The Erotic Object: Sexuality in Sculpture From Prehistory to the Present Day
Sex in Art: Pornography and Pleasure in Painting and Sculpture
Postwar Art
Sacred Gardens: The Garden in Myth, Religion and Art
Glorification: Religious Abstraction in Renaissance and 20th Century Art
Early Netherlandish Painting
Leonardo da Vinci
Piero della Francesca
Giovanni Bellini
Fra Angelico: Art and Religion in the Renaissance
Mark Rothko: The Art of Transcendence
Frank Stella: American Abstract Artist
Jasper Johns
Brice Marden
Alison Wilding: The Embrace of Sculpture
Vincent van Gogh: Visionary Landscapes
Eric Gill: Nuptials of God
Constantin Brancusi: Sculpting the Essence of Things
Max Beckmann
Caravaggio
Gustave Moreau
Egon Schiele: Sex and Death In Purple Stockings
Delizioso Fotografico Fervore: Works In Process 1
Sacro Cuore: Works In Process 2
The Light Eternal: J.M.W. Turner
The Madonna Glorified: Karen Arthurs

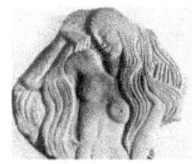

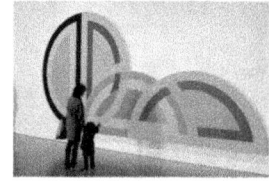

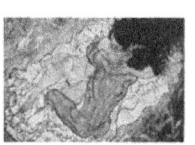

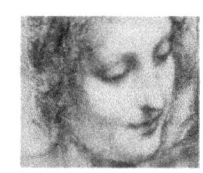

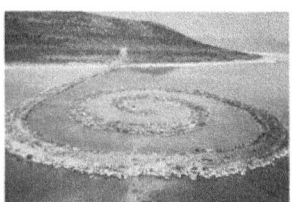

LITERATURE

J.R.R. Tolkien: The Books, The Films, The Whole Cultural Phenomenon
J.R.R. Tolkien: Pocket Guide
Tolkien's Heroic Quest
The *Earthsea* Books of Ursula Le Guin
Beauties, Beasts and Enchantment: Classic French Fairy Tales
German Popular Stories by the Brothers Grimm
Philip Pullman and *His Dark Materials*
Sexing Hardy: Thomas Hardy and Feminism
Thomas Hardy's *Tess of the d'Urbervilles*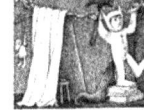
Thomas Hardy's *Jude the Obscure*
Thomas Hardy: The Tragic Novels
Love and Tragedy: Thomas Hardy
The Poetry of Landscape in Hardy
Wessex Revisited: Thomas Hardy and John Cowper Powys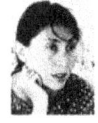
Wolfgang Iser: Essays and Interviews
Petrarch, Dante and the Troubadours
Maurice Sendak and the Art of Children's Book Illustration
Andrea Dworkin
Cixous, Irigaray, Kristeva: The *Jouissance* of French Feminism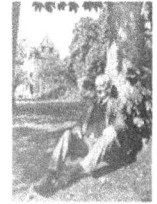
Julia Kristeva: Art, Love, Melancholy, Philosophy, Semiotics and Psychoanalysis
Hélene Cixous I Love You: The *Jouissance* of Writing
Luce Irigaray: Lips, Kissing, and the Politics of Sexual Difference
Peter Redgrove: Here Comes the Flood
Peter Redgrove: Sex-Magic-Poetry-Cornwall
Lawrence Durrell: Between Love and Death, East and West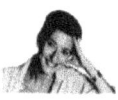
Love, Culture & Poetry: Lawrence Durrell
Cavafy: Anatomy of a Soul
German Romantic Poetry: Goethe, Novalis, Heine, Hölderlin
Feminism and Shakespeare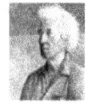
Shakespeare: Love, Poetry & Magic
The Passion of D.H. Lawrence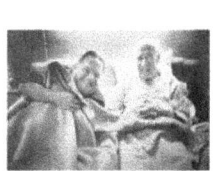
D.H. Lawrence: Symbolic Landscapes
D.H. Lawrence: Infinite Sensual Violence
Rimbaud: Arthur Rimbaud and the Magic of Poetry
The Ecstasies of John Cowper Powys
Sensualism and Mythology: The Wessex Novels of John Cowper Powys
Amorous Life: John Cowper Powys and the Manifestation of Affectivity (H.W. Fawkner)
Postmodern Powys: New Essays on John Cowper Powys (Joe Boulter)
Rethinking Powys: Critical Essays on John Cowper Powys
Paul Bowles & Bernardo Bertolucci
Rainer Maria Rilke
Joseph Conrad: *Heart of Darkness*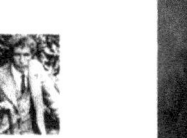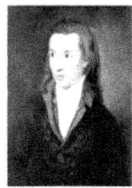
In the Dim Void: Samuel Beckett
Samuel Beckett Goes into the Silence
André Gide: Fiction and Fervour
Jackie Collins and the Blockbuster Novel
Blinded By Her Light: The Love-Poetry of Robert Graves
The Passion of Colours: Travels In Mediterranean Lands
Poetic Forms

POETRY

Ursula Le Guin: Walking In Cornwall
Peter Redgrove: Here Comes The Flood
Peter Redgrove: Sex-Magic-Poetry-Cornwall
Dante: Selections From the Vita Nuova
Petrarch, Dante and the Troubadours
William Shakespeare: Sonnets
William Shakespeare: Complete Poems
Blinded By Her Light: The Love-Poetry of Robert Graves
Emily Dickinson: Selected Poems
Emily Brontë: Poems
Thomas Hardy: Selected Poems
Percy Bysshe Shelley: Poems
John Keats: Selected Poems
Joh n Keats: Poems of 1820
D.H. Lawrence: Selected Poems
Edmund Spenser: Poems
Edmund Spenser: Amoretti
John Donne: Poems
Henry Vaughan: Poems
Sir Thomas Wyatt: Poems
Robert Herrick: Selected Poems
Rilke: Space, Essence and Angels in the Poetry of Rainer Maria Rilke
Rainer Maria Rilke: Selected Poems
Friedrich Hölderlin: Selected Poems
Arseny Tarkovsky: Selected Poems
Arthur Rimbaud: Selected Poems
Arthur Rimbaud: A Season in Hell
Arthur Rimbaud and the Magic of Poetry
Novalis: Hymns To the Night
German Romantic Poetry
Paul Verlaine: Selected Poems
Elizaethan Sonnet Cycles
D.J. Enright: By-Blows
Jeremy Reed: Brigitte's Blue Heart
Jeremy Reed: Claudia Schiffer's Red Shoes
Gorgeous Little Orpheus
Radiance: New Poems
Crescent Moon Book of Nature Poetry
Crescent Moon Book of Love Poetry
Crescent Moon Book of Mystical Poetry
Crescent Moon Book of Elizabethan Love Poetry
Crescent Moon Book of Metaphysical Poetry
Crescent Moon Book of Romantic Poetry
Pagan America: New American Poetry

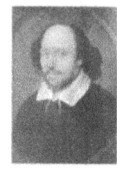
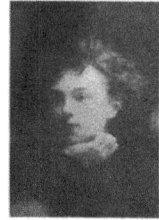
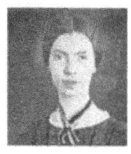
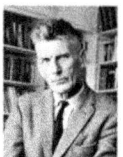

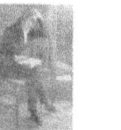
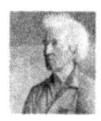
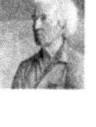
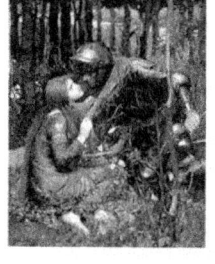
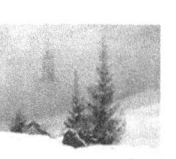
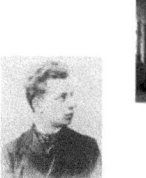
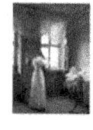

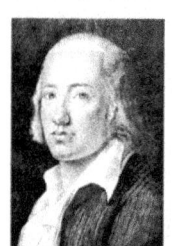
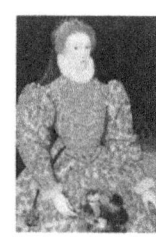

MEDIA, CINEMA, FEMINISM and CULTURAL STUDIES

J.R.R. Tolkien: The Books, The Films, The Whole Cultural Phenomenon
J.R.R. Tolkien: Pocket Guide
The *Lord of the Rings* Movies: Pocket Guide
The Cinema of Hayao Miyazaki
Hayao Miyazaki: *Princess Mononoke*: Pocket Movie Guide
Hayao Miyazaki: *Spirited Away*: Pocket Movie Guide

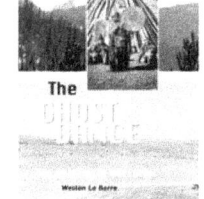

Tim Burton : Hallowe'en For Hollywood
Ken Russell
Ken Russell: *Tommy*: Pocket Movie Guide
The Ghost Dance: The Origins of Religion
The Peyote Cult
Cixous, Irigaray, Kristeva: The *Jouissance* of French Feminism
Julia Kristeva: Art, Love, Melancholy, Philosophy, Semiotics and Psychoanalysis
Luce Irigaray: Lips, Kissing, and the Politics of Sexual Difference
Hélene Cixous I Love You: The *Jouissance* of Writing
Andrea Dworkin
'Cosmo Woman': The World of Women's Magazines
Women in Pop Music
HomeGround: The Kate Bush Anthology
Discovering the Goddess (Geoffrey Ashe)
The Poetry of Cinema
The Sacred Cinema of Andrei Tarkovsky
Andrei Tarkovsky: Pocket Guide
Andrei Tarkovsky: *Mirror*: Pocket Movie Guide
Andrei Tarkovsky: *The Sacrifice*: Pocket Movie Guide
Walerian Borowczyk: Cinema of Erotic Dreams
Jean-Luc Godard: The Passion of Cinema
Jean-Luc Godard: *Hail Mary*: Pocket Movie Guide
Jean-Luc Godard: *Contempt*: Pocket Movie Guide
Jean-Luc Godard: *Pierrot le Fou*: Pocket Movie Guide
John Hughes and Eighties Cinema
Ferris Bueller's Day Off: Pocket Movie Guide
Jean-Luc Godard: Pocket Guide
The Cinema of Richard Linklater
Liv Tyler: Star In Ascendance
Blade Runner and the Films of Philip K. Dick
Paul Bowles and Bernardo Bertolucci
Media Hell: Radio, TV and the Press
An Open Letter to the BBC
Detonation Britain: Nuclear War in the UK
Feminism and Shakespeare
Wild Zones: Pornography, Art and Feminism
Sex in Art: Pornography and Pleasure in Painting and Sculpture
Sexing Hardy: Thomas Hardy and Feminism

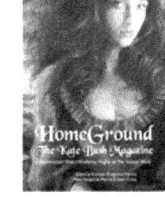
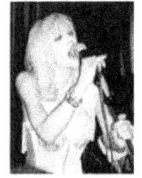
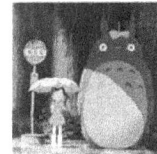
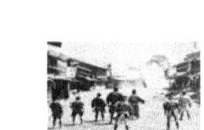

The Light Eternal is a model monograph, an exemplary job. The subject matter of the book is beautifully
organised and dead on beam. (Lawrence Durrell)
It is amazing for me to see my work treated with such passion and respect. (Andrea Dworkin)

CRESCENT MOON PUBLISHING
P.O. Box 1312, Maidstone, Kent, ME14 5XU, Great Britain. www.crmoon.com

cresmopub@yahoo.co.uk   www.crescentmoon.org.uk

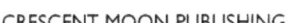